MISSED YOU

ROBYN REED

THE SWEETWATER SERIES

This book is a work of fiction. Names, characters, venues, and incidents are the products of the author's imagination or used fictitiously. Any resemblance to the actual events locales or persons, living or dead is entirely coincidental.

ACKNOWLEDGMENTS

To my husband Jacob. Thank you for supporting my dreams every day.

Thank you to all of my wonderful family, friends and clients who have believed in me and encouraged me to turn my hobby into a dream, especially those clients who have helped with the editing and proof reading of my first book. I will forever be grateful.

AUTHORS NOTE

Missed you, book 1 of 3 in the Sweetwater Series, is the first in what will eventually be a long line of series. My books all have a lot of spice and a happy ending, as I myself can't read a book without one.

So, if you enjoy a slightly possessive alpha male and a good love story with a little drama sprinkled in, you've come to the right place.

Enjoy reading. X

TABLE OF CONTENTS

1

Grace

I shouldn't be doing this on my Saturday evening.

I should be sitting in my apartment with a good book and a glass of wine. But no. It's currently 8pm on a rainy September evening, and I'm standing on the front porch of my two best friends' house they share and have done since we left college. My best friend's Rose, Hallie and Me, have known each other since we were just six years old. Trying to figure each other out in the school playground on our first day, the three of us have been pretty much inseparable ever since.

After we all attended the same college together, I decided it was time to leave my hometown in Sweetwater and see what was out there. Find something, I could do with my accounting degree. That was until yesterday afternoon, when I came home from work early, and found my boyfriend balls deep in the neighbour from two doors down. Cindy, *ugh*. That tacky blonde who always has her boobs pushed up around her neck, and a skirt so short you can't leave much to the imagination.

I guess it was just enough for Liam though. My now *ex*-boyfriend Liam and I had been together for almost two years, and this weekend I was planning on surprising him with a trip to Mexico for the week to spend some much needed quality time together. Guess the jokes on me though, as he admitted they had been sleeping together for just short of 6 months.

He didn't even seem the least bit bothered by the fact I was standing gawping at them for a good minute, before he finally turned his stupid head and saw me. I kicked them both out and bolted the door shut, before I allowed myself a whole 10 minutes to be sad and cry. Any more than that and it was a waste.

The relationship we had wasn't passion filled or exciting. No, it was easy.. comfortable. We'd met whilst he was at work sorting an IT problem at the office in Atlanta, and he had asked me out for a drink. He was easy on the eye and could turn on the charm with his blue eyes and shaggy blonde hair.

Guess that was how Cindy fell into his lap one afternoon, when he told me he was going to fix her laptop for her. God I was such an idiot not to have seen it. But that was then, and now, after an almost 6 hour drive, I'm standing in front of Hallie and Rose's house, trying to figure out what to say to my girls.

Reaching up I hit the knocker a couple of times, and I'm only waiting at the door for all of five seconds when it swings open and my gorgeous best friend Rose is standing looking at me like I have two heads. That must be what happens when you turn up unannounced on their doorstep. She blinks at me a couple of times like she can't quite figure out if it's really me she's looking at, until it finally must register in her head when she launches herself at me and pulls me into the biggest most comforting hug, that makes me just want to cry.

I let myself hug her back for a quick second whilst I gather my thoughts and tell her why I'm on her door at a stupid time but she beats me to it.

"What the hell are you doing here Grace? I wasn't expecting to see you until Thanksgiving".

She pulls back and looks at me with her freckled face, auburn hair pulled up into a messy pile on her head and her curious hazel eyes searching back at me for the answer. Fuck it, just come out with it Grace.

"I caught Liam in bed with Cindy from a few doors down, and I.. I didn't know where else to come to, so here I am.." She looks at me with pure shock and anger on her face "What an absolute asshole, I'm gonna bury him!"

Well, I didn't quite expect that reaction but we'll roll with it.

"Rose chill, I know you're a secret psychopath but, I don't think we should unalive him for the time being".

Rose looks back at me and scoffs, assessing my face once more. Before she spins around and holler's me into her place as I follow her in with my small overnight bag flung over my shoulder that I packed with essentials, because I wasn't routing for my toothbrush in the several bin bags I had stashed in my car this late in the evening. She shows me to the guest room with my own bathroom. The walls are pretty simple in an off white, oak floor with a rug lining the underneath of the bed which is neatly made up with white sheets. The other side of the room has a dressing table with a corner chair and a small wardrobe off to the side. It's dark out now though so I have yet to discover my view from my window. It’s such a cosy house and I say cosy lightly, as the place is huge and absolutely gorgeous.

Built about 6 years ago it's on a super quiet street, with lofty ceilings and white walls. The living area is a comfortable size with a huge corner suite you can just fall into, a love seat to the other side and tv above the modern fireplace. Bright pops of colour are dotted all over the place with cushions and artwork, so it's not too clinical. The open plan feature lets you see into the state-of-the-art kitchen Hallie's dad, Jerry had put in for them.

He’s the local joiner in the next town over with his own company that Hallie currently works for, as she couldn't find anything in her field she was happy with. Beyond the kitchen, the glass back to the house looks down onto the lake, with a dock leading up to it. It's a beautiful home that Hallie and Rose got lucky enough to snag, as her dad did a lot of work with the building of them. And now I'm here to figure out what the hell I'm going to do with my life, since it got turned upside down just over 24 hours ago.

“Right, now you are settled in, what’s the plan?” Rose asks as she hands me a glass of white wine and plops herself down onto the love seat in the corner, whilst I lounge on the sofa. “Urgh” I groan, “I don't even know. I've told work I need to take personal time and explained what happened to Andy. He told me to take all the time I need”.

My boss Andy is literally the best boss I could have asked for. When I called him first thing and told him that Liam and I had split up and I needed some time away from the office, he told me not to worry, but to take my laptop and work from home.. I'm not sure he meant my hometown home, but it's the best he's getting for now.

"Ok, so you're free to stay here as long as you like. We definitely have the space and.. EEK!! I'm so excited that you're back for a while, or for good? Either way, Hallie will be really excited when she gets back. She's gone to get dinner for us, so you'll see her in about 20 minutes", she rambles on in her own little world as she attempts to put my whole life together for me.

"Rose, I think I'll have to move back here for a while, I can't stay in the same city as him. He literally goes everywhere I go; I wouldn't be able to escape him."

Rose makes an exaggerated shiver and crosses her eyes before blurting out, "Ugh what an absolute creeper. Did he not let you go anywhere by yourself? Sounds like it was a good thing he did what he's done girl. You're better off here with us, and I'm pretty sure my dad is looking for a new head accountant at the office. Patricia retired last week and he's going mad having to rely on the newbies. But I know you, and you are the smartest woman I know".

"Hey I thought that was me!" Hallie says with a grin on her face, as she comes fumbling into the kitchen area. Her hands piled high with Chinese food. Once she's set it down, she turns to me with the biggest, most genuine smile on her face.

Her mid-length blonde hair is falling in big waves down her back and her cheeks are a little pink from the rain and cold air outside. "Grace babe, when did you get in? Is this a flying visit or do you have some time off?"

I look at my friend shyly, as I realise I've just crashed at her place without even checking it was ok with *both* friends first. I love Rose and Hallie equally, but Rose wouldn't say no to anyone short of an axe murderer wanting to stop over, so of course she would invite me into their home without checking with Hallie first.

"She's here for the long-haul girl, set her up in the guest bedroom", Rose says, hiking a thumb over her shoulder in the direction of the bedrooms. "That asshole of an ex had his dick in Cindy down the hall and gave her the push she needed to come back to us. I didn't ring you because I knew you would be cool with it." Rose pipes up from the kitchen, where she's now digging her head into the food they clearly over ordered.

Hallie's brown eyes sparkle as she looks over to me, she looks like she could cry right now as she walks right over to me where I'm lounging on the couch, climbs on with me, and smothers me in a hug. At 5"10 she has a figure like a supermodel, all legs that go on for days. Her tall frame towers over me as she wraps her body around my smaller, 5"7 curvy body into a tight hug. Considering she is so slim, she knows how to comfort, and her lavender scent soothes me as it takes over my senses.

Hallie is the mother of the group, whilst Rose is the chatty slightly crazy one and I'm the geeky book-worm. I'm not really sure how we stayed friends for this long, but I guess the mixture of our personalities was just the right combination. We've rarely had disagreements and if we did, they were quickly sorted by mother hen.

"Well, in that case, welcome back girl. Stay as long as you like. Or if you're moving back home for good then I have to say, I'm even happier about that."

I wince as I think about my answer. "I think I'll be here for good, so long as I find a job to pay my way. I'm not sure my boss would be happy with me working remotely on a permanent basis. Plus, I need normality, and that will not happen if I have to work from home for the foreseeable. I'll go see your dad on Monday Rose, see if he can give me an interview."

"No need" she says as she waves her phone at me. "Texting him now to let him know you're here and can fill the job. He wants to know your earliest start date." I look over to her, a frown tugging at my brow "Jesus Rose. Give a girl a minute" her freckled face scowls back at me, noodles on her fork in one hand, and phone in the other. "Hey, I'm not giving you a chance to back out and go back to Atlanta. You are back here to stay, and that's that". *Christ this girl*. I roll my eyes at her whilst trying to hide my smile, but I'm just so happy to be here and not moping around my old place where I'll most likely bump into *them.*

"Have you called your parents and told them you're back yet?" Hallie asks from beside me where she's still smoothing over my hair with her hands.

"Erm.. no. I need to figure out what to say to them. You know what my dad is like. He'll go after him with a shotgun given half the chance, and I don't need my mom's pitying looks. They both mean well, but you know how overbearing they are with me being the baby, and the only one to have left town".

I love both of my parents to death. But at the ages of fifty-five and sixty, my mom and dad have coddled me so much since I was little. My older brother and sister, Tristan and Lily have it easy.. He's taking over from my dad on the ranch they own, and Lily is a stay at home mom who runs around after her kids, and being the middle child, she somehow always gets the most attention.

My parents thought I would stay here and settle down with one of the boys from town, and that's what they are.. Boys. Other than the one I left here because I knew I didn't stand a chance with him, I needed to find myself someone I thought was different from the rest. How wrong was I. "Ugh," I groan into the cushion, "Why can't I just have a simple life with no drama for once".

"Fat chance of that buttercup. Now come get food before it either gets cold, or I eat it all." Rose shouts back to me from where she has now perched herself on one of the stools that line the marble island in the kitchen.

Hallie and I mock salute her, but we get up from the sofa to grab food and settle down for the night devouring way too much and eventually, even more wine. We chat and catch up some more about Rose's job, and how much Hallie wants to find something where she's back being a nanny of some sort, we eventually wear each other out with the chatter, and by the end of the evening when I climb into bed, I'm feeling slightly less apprehensive about how much my life is about to change. I just hope it's for the better.

2

Grace

Sunday morning, I wake up with a start, momentarily forgetting where I am and have a panic. I look around the room figuring out my surroundings as the last two days of my shambles of a life comes flooding back, and I throw my head back into my pillow letting out a loud groan. I sit up after a minute looking out of the window which is conveniently placed at the bottom end of my bed, where the sun has come out and cleared the rain from the past week. It beams down onto the lake with not a cloud in the sky, if only the inside of my brain was as clear as that.

I decide to give myself 10 minutes to collect my thoughts, before dragging myself out of bed and into the bathroom, wincing at the sight of myself. My long ebony hair is sticking out all over the place, having slipped out of my scrunchie through the night, and my makeup still mars my face, with the bags under my eyes that could carry a shop load they're that big.

With a sigh I straighten my hair out and clear my face of my remaining makeup, brush my teeth and head downstairs for coffee. But when I get to the kitchen, Hallie is already sitting in her shorts and sports bra, sweat running down her back and a glowy sheen to her face, her blonde hair is pulled into a tight pony on top of her head. I'm guessing she's been on her usual morning run. *Jeez,* how late did I sleep in, quickly glancing at the clock on the oven though I realise it's only 9am, so I know I've not slept the day away. "Good morning sunshine".

Ugh she's too chipper for this time on a Sunday, I grunt my response to her and trudge over to the coffee machine to make myself a mug.

Once I have some caffeine in my system and I finally feel like I can actually muster up some conversation, I turn to my friend to attempt to be social "You're up early for a Sunday, did you fall out of bed or something?" She chuckles into her coffee before giving me the side eye a slight smirk.

"The neighbour does a run with a couple of his friends on a Sunday morning, and I hate to pass up the opportunity to show off my running skills.. And for the perv of course". I snort into my coffee at my friend's bluntness. Hallie doesn't struggle for male attention. Her blonde hair, bronzed skin and girl next door attitude makes every guy fall over themselves for her. She knows she's a knockout but doesn't flaunt it or make herself seem better than everyone else. A trait I love about her.

"Oh! You should come with me; it will do you good to get out there and find yourself a new man to get under". She says winking at me with a look on her face that makes me think she's about to drag me into the worst idea she might have ever had.

"Absolutely not. Nuh uh. No way. I do not need any man right now. I've had enough drama for one lifetime. I'll stick with my little rubber pal, thank you" I return pointing my nose up at her before I take another sip of my coffee, but as I peer back over at her, her eyes are sparkling with mischief, and with that look I know nothing good for my sanity can come of it.

"Well then, I'll let you stew this week, I get it's been a heavy weekend but next week we are going out. And don't even think of trying to get out of it. We haven't seen you in forever and we need a girl's night" she says pouting at me from over the kitchen counter, but the sternness to her voice lets me know she means business. "Ok, ok. fine. I'll humour you for one night and then leave me alone so I can fester".

"Yey" she almost shouts, bouncing about in her seat like an excited little toddler, her blonde hair bouncing in her ponytail.

……..

By the time the afternoon rolls around, I have gathered up enough courage to go and speak to my mom and dad, making my presence known back at home. Looking at my watch it's reading just after 1pm, so dad should be finishing up and getting ready for Sunday dinner with the family. Everyone comes to our parents for Sunday dinner every week, well except me of course, but that's all about to change as I step onto the porch and knock on the front door.

My parent’s place is an old blue and white farmhouse, with a wrap-around porch and a couple of acres for the horses that my dad trains and sells. The chickens and llamas, which my mom bought without telling dad and is adamant on keeping, are milling about making too much noise for my liking, but she loves them probably more than the three children she raised. The two golden retrievers, Amber and Whiskey, which they got just before I moved away come running up to the front door. Happily yapping at me like greeting an old friend.

“Coming” my mom shouts from what sounds like the back of the house, and a minute later she’s standing in front of me, her features swirling with a mix of shock and excitement as she takes me in. She's wearing her Sunday favourite, a purple wrap dress covered by her cooking apron and a towel slung over her shoulder. “Grace darling, when did you get here? Are you staying for dinner, there's plenty to go around”. She waffles as she wraps me in a hug and I melt into her as her warmth takes over my body, helping to ease that bit of anxiety I had about coming here today.

“Yeah mom, I'm staying. For um.. a while actually. I'm staying with Rose and Hallie at their place, until I decide what I want to do. It's a long story but me and Liam are no longer together, and so I've decided to come back home, indefinitely”. She squeezes me tighter at that, and I know she's happy to have me back. “Oh baby. I'm sorry to hear about you and Liam. But I am most definitely glad you are back home”. Thankfully she leaves it there for now, and we walk into the house. Neither of my siblings are here yet, allowing me the opportunity to relax in the kitchen whilst I wait for my dad to appear. Mom hands me a glass of wine whilst she's cooking and fills me in with what she's been up to since we last spoke. Whilst she's chatting away, I take time to look around me at the house that I grew up in. The kitchen hasn't been updated in at least fifteen years, but it has the classic farmhouse style kitchen that still looks like it would fit into a modern house today.

It's a big enough room that the large oak dining table also fits in here which I have noticed is already plated up for 9 people, which I find odd since there's only 8 usually, so I wait to ask her who else is coming for dinner when she comes up for air.

My train of thought is cut short by my dad barrelling into the kitchen whistling in singsong. He saddles up beside my mom, wraps his arms around her waist and gives her a peck on the cheek, to which she giggles at him. It's only when he realizes she's chatting away does he look up to see me watching them together.

"My baby is home" he all but cries, as he comes over to me, picking me up and into his signature bear hug, squeezing me just a little too tightly. "Hi daddy, I missed you so much" I say, squeezing him back. He might be 60 years old but he's still very strong and well-built for a man of his age.

At a little over 6ft tall, sharp jaw and his full head of salt and pepper hair with a broad build, my dad looks like he could be on a lumberjack advert. He's adorning his usual attire of a checked shirt, Wrangler jeans and a pair of boots, and it's no wonder that my mom still looks at him the way she does. Seeing pictures of him and her back in the day, they were the ultimate couple. My mom, who's a few years younger than him, still looks youthful as ever, like not a day over 45 with a killer figure, and just a little shorter than him at 5ft7. Her blonde bobbed hair, which comes to just beneath her chin is highlighted with streaks of silver that look like they were done at the salon. She's wearing a little eye makeup, which makes her blue eyes pop, helped by the golden glow on her skin from spending time outside.

My sister and I take after my dad's side with our dark hair, green eyes that have flecks of amber in them, and a creamy complexion. We share his pouty lips, but our other features are our mother. Warm smiles, and curvy figures and just as I'm thinking about my sister, she appears in the doorway holding the smallest of her 4 children. At 30, she's been married to her childhood sweetheart, Henley for ten years now. They married young as they both wanted to have a big family and she certainly got what she asked for when she had her children.

Their eldest is eight-year-old Brody, who is the most perfect boy I could have ever seen when I first laid eyes on him. Gangly legs, showing that he's going to be tall like his dad when he's older. Paired with his soft personality which just melts your heart every time you speak to him. She had the shock of her life when the next two popped out together at once. Her girls, Mia and Jessica who are 5, are typical girly girls that have themselves wrapped tightly around Henley's little finger, and wallet. Then along came the baby. Max, who is only ten months old and already has a cheeky personality, keeps the whole family on their toes.

My sister beams at me from across the room when she spots me. There are three years between us, but we are like best friends. I used to enjoy winding her up when we were younger, but then I got into maths and mellowed out as she says. Once she's crossed the kitchen and rounded the island to get to me, she hugs me with one arm so that she doesn't squish baby Max, who coos and grabs at my hair with his chubby little fists. I reach over for him, pulling him out of her arms and start blowing raspberries on his cheeks and he returns a gurgled laugh and nuzzles into me.

"Thanks for the heads up you were coming home sis". Lily scolds from where she has moved over to the fridge. "Sorry I thought you might like the surprise" I return with a shrug of my shoulder hoping she doesn't ask questions. At that moment, her three other children come running into the room, the girls squabbling over a doll whilst Henley battles to separate them and Brody follows behind, head in a science book. "Girls carry on and you can both sit in the field with the chickens instead of enjoying dinner with the rest of us… And look, Auntie Grace has come to visit. Wouldn't want to miss out on that would you?"

Hearing that, both of their heads instantly snap up to meet mine and they squeal in delight running over to wrap themselves around my legs. I let out a small laugh, whilst Henley also lets Brody know I'm here. He holds back while the girls say their hello's and then comes to my side to give me a squeeze. "Gosh

Brody, you are getting too big, you need to stop growing". He just rolls his eyes at me smiling and replies with "That's because I'm growing up to be big and strong like my daddy".

"That's right kiddo. You're going to be as big and tall as me by the time you're ten the rate you are growing at!" Henley says as he joins his wife's side.

Whilst we are waiting for dinner to finish cooking and my brother to arrive, we all head out into the back garden so the kids can all enjoy the sunshine. The older 3 run off to the tree house that my dad built us when we were their age, and Max crawls around picking at daisies he finds in the ground. I sit playing with Max whilst mom and Lily catch up about their day, whilst my dad and Henley head over to the tree house to keep an eye on the kids, both with a beer in hand.

After about twenty minutes I hear what must be my brother's truck pull up to the house and a couple of minutes later he opens up the back door and steps into the garden. As he walks over to us, I stand up to greet him, and he spots me instantly, making his way over to wrap me in a hug "Good to see you home Grace", he says as he releases me.

But the air leaves my lungs, and I'm pretty sure my heart stops beating, when I hear the voice that I longed for, for far too long. Sleepless nights wishing he were mine instead of whoever he had keeping his bed warm at the time. My silly teenage crush that I could just never seem to shake. That deep sexy voice that purrs when he says my name, and I know I'm a goner all over again.

“Hey Grace, it's been too long”.

Apparently not long enough for me, because as my brother grins and turns back to his best friend, I go a little weak at the knees when I come face to face with my lifelong crush.

Jaxx Archer.

3

Grace

“Jaxx honey, I'm really glad you could make it” my mom says as she gets to her feet to greet him. He hugs her, and even entertains her kissing him on the cheek, whilst my dad is next to approach him gripping his hand in a firm shake, and whilst he's distracted, I quickly grip a hold of my brother's arm and angrily whisper in his ear, “Since when does Jaxx come for fucking Sunday dinners?” He glances back to me with a puzzled look on his face, clearly not getting why I'm so pissed right now, and nudges his arm out of my grip whilst shaking his head at me, “Get a grip of yourself Grace. He comes every week for dinner when he's not working. I would have given you prior notice, but you decided to show up unannounced”. I scowl at him trying to see if I can figure out more information about Jaxx without looking like a creep. “Does he not prefer to spend his Sundays with his girlfriend or something?”

Tristan barks out a laugh at me, causing everyone to turn and look at us. I go beet red and move to hide my face from Jaxx's eye line, and when my brother finally brings his face back to mine, I narrow my eyes on him. His eyes crinkle slightly in the corner as he smiles making him look at lot fucking older than he's acting right now, and I decide I don't have the patience for this anymore, so I stomp over to my sister hoping she can give me some insight.

She's messing around with Max on the floor, so I crouch down to her level whilst trying to keep my voice down, “Tristan said Jaxx comes for dinner every week, why do you so conveniently miss that out of the conversation when I call you”. Her head whips up to meet my gaze and her eyes do the same crinkle as Tristan’s when she smiles back at me, *this fucking family of mine.* “Don't know what you're talking about Grace, and you said you didn't want to hear about him, I've gotta go change Max's diaper, so I’ll see you inside, yeah?” She walks off from me before I even get a chance to say another word to her, leaving me standing like an idiot watching Jaxx deep in conversation with my dad and Henley.

The air feels like it has disappeared from around me, silently suffocating me as I drink him in. Long legs clad with a pair of blue Levi jeans, that I'm sure would hug his ass to perfection, if he just turned a little to the side so I could get a peek. A white tee on his top half that shows off those muscular arms, leaving nothing to the imagination as to just how much he has been working out recently. When the hell did he get so *big?* My eyes eventually move up to scan over his face, which seems to have just gotten more masculine and somehow even more beautiful all at once the older he has gotten.

His stubble frames his pouty lips, nose with a slight bump in it where he broke it a few times when we were younger. And steely grey eyes that are staring back at me with a smirk now tugging at his lips. *Shit,* he definitely just caught me eye fucking him.

I can't help it though when he just looks so fucking good. *Stop it Grace, you are meant to be over him!* I pull my gaze away from his as I feel the heat creep up my throat from being caught in the act, and he excuses himself from the conversation with my dad and brother-in-law to come and greet me, and as he approaches me his presence heats my overly hot body even more than it already is. He still smells exactly the same as I remember, a mix of pine and sandalwood invading my nostrils as he leans in to pull me into a hug, his warm minty breath fanning my face as he presses his lips to my ear.

“Missed you baby girl. It's about time you came home”. I pull back scowling at him and search his face for any explanation of the name, but all he does is tighten his grip on my waist and smile like I'm his favourite person in the world. *Fuck, fuck.*

When he finally pulls away from me, I look him up and down trying to get a gauge on him, but my mom calls us into dinner, pulling him from me a little more. He turns to walk into the house, but not before sneaking a look over his shoulder to give me a final glance up and down and shooting me a wink with a satisfied look on his face.

Fuck! How am I supposed to get through this dinner, when all I'm now thinking about is how good he looks. His ass is definitely sculpted to perfection, which he seems to be giving me a show of as I watch him walk back into the house. My panties are now a little… No, a lot damp after he just called me *Baby girl* and showed me that fine ass.

I have to give myself a minute to cool off and catch my breath again before steeling myself and following everyone inside the house for lunch. Looking around the table when I enter the kitchen, I go to take a seat next to my nephew, but I'm quickly stopped by Tristan. "I'm sitting with Brody today Grace, we have to catch up talking about his baseball game at the weekend, don't we Brody?" Brody's little face fills with a bright smile as he responds to his uncle with a quick nod, and I'm left staring at the only seat left, right next to Jaxx. *God fucking help me.*

Jaxx looks up to me, a slight twitch to his lips as he reaches over and pats the seat next to him. "Come on Grace. Saved you a seat next to me, I'm sure we have a lot to catch up on".

I give him a shy smile as those eyes follow me around the table and I come to stand next to him. But before I can grab the chair, he's up and out of his seat pulling my chair out for me. I don't know what the hell is going on with him today, but he needs to cut it out. I left this place for a reason, and that reason is currently making my heart thud a thousand miles an hour, so I do what I know best and give him a slight scowl but not forgetting my manners. "Thank you Jaxx, you didn't need to do that". He leans in closer to me once he has taken his seat and murmurs "Anything for you, Baby Girl".

Oh my god. Nope. Just stop. I lean away from him as much as I can trying to distract myself whilst talking to my sister from across the table, but the heat

I can feel coming off his body is too much. Every now and again he brushes his arm against mine whilst reaching for food, all whilst his chair is most definitely too close to mine. I can feel his thigh rubbing up against mine each time he shifts slightly and the heat from him is making my panties more wet just at the thought of him. All the things he could do to me right now, with those corded arms and long fingers that… Nope. No. *DO NOT go there Grace.*

I inwardly cringe at myself and my dirty thoughts, or I think I do but I must not do a very good job because my sister gives me a funny look, which I return with a wry smile, as she carries on the conversation which my mum has now joined in on.

"So Grace, what's the reason for the surprise visit you have sprung upon us?" my brother asks from across the table while all my family's eyes turn to me expectantly, waiting for me to give them an answer. It's only when my brain finally kicks into gear that I take a breath and prepare myself for the truth.

"I found Liam cheating on me with the neighbour, and I.. I just couldn't stay there at the risk of bumping into them, and so I've decided to move back here. It's just easier this way because I don't know what I might do if I see him right now". I suck in a breath as I see Jaxx tense up a little out of the corner of my eye, but I ignore him and continue "I packed up as much as I could and high tailed it to Rose and Hallie's, they have taken me in and said I can live with them".

The breath I was holding on to pours out of me after dropping that bomb on my family, and as I glance down again I spot Jaxx clenching his fists that hard his knuckles are turning white, causing me to look up at him, where his jaw is set tight like he's trying to hold something in. Huh. When I look over to my brother though, his face has morphed into pure rage and after a moment of letting it build, he shoves his chair back to stand, pacing the kitchen floor whilst ranting. "How fucking *dare* he hurt you like this. That piece of shit, I'm going to drive there myself to make sure he knows he fucked with the wrong person".

I hold up my hand to stop him in his tracks. "No Tristan. You won't do anything of the sort. What's done is done, and I can't change what's happened so we need to leave it at that". My brother rears his head back like I've just slapped him, shock evident in his face that I've had the audacity to stop him getting into any more trouble than he has over the years.

I roll my eyes at his dramatics and continue, "I'm back for as long as I need to be, until I decide what I am doing with my job. Rose's dad has said there is a job at his firm for me but I need to figure out if I want to stay here for the long haul". He shakes head but sits back down to try and calm himself.

My dad doesn't stay quiet for long though before he comes out his usual bluntness. "Well, I for one am glad that you dumped his sorry ass, because I never liked him anyway". Jaxx barely stifles a laugh beside me whilst my mom scolds my dad, "Harold. Do not say things like that, what if they work through things."

"Absolutely not fucking happening", Jaxx murmurs beside me and I wonder if he thinks I didn't catch it, but the look in his eyes tells me he would go to great lengths to keep Liam from trying to get me back. My brother seems to agree with him, like he heard him too as he joins back in again being his overbearing self. “Over my dead body is she going anywhere near him or that place. Grace, if you need to go back there either me, Jaxx or Henley needs to be with you because I don’t trust the guy. Always thought he was a snake, and now he goes and does this to you.” Jaxx and Henley just nod in agreement and I let out a long sigh trying to think how to put a stop to the conversation, “Alright can we get off this topic now guys, I've had enough drama for one weekend.”

Thankfully my nieces swerve the conversation to safer pastures, and dinner continues at a safe level, but still does little to calm the anxiety building in me. I feel like I could settle back in here, providing Liam stays out of my life like I need him to.. but I don't want to worry about that right now and so I focus on the meal and settle back and try for the rest of the time to be involved in the family chat and out of my own head. But the whole way through dinner, all I can feel is Jaxx's gaze on me.

4

Jaxx

I need to get out of this house to cool down before I say something stupid. My head feels like it's about to explode whilst I try to figure out what the hell to do with this situation. I kept tabs on Grace whilst she was in Atlanta, but clearly not enough to know that the asshole was sleeping with someone behind her back. I suppose that comes as a perk of being the town Sheriff, I have everything I need at my fingertips, and that includes keeping Grace safe even if it is from afar. And now.. now she's back in town and I intend to do everything I can from letting her slip out of my life again.

Grace clearly needed to do some soul searching whilst she was away, but I didn't expect her to actually enjoy being away so much and not want to return. Five years is a damn long time, the amount of time since I last saw her, not that I was counting or anything, but wow has it done her some favours. Her body has filled out beautifully over the years. Perfect hourglass figure she shows off without even realising it, with skintight leggings and a cropped hoodie frame her perfect waist, hips and that ass.

Damn, she has definitely grown up a lot from the twenty-one-year-old that left me all those years ago. I, for sure thought I'd lost her for good when she got with *him,* and I tried to move on myself but nothing stuck. I feel like I probably should have told her how I felt before she left, but I knew she'd hate the idea and reject me, especially since her brother is my best friend, and has been since we were just kids. But we are grown-ups now, and I'm not prepared to sit on the side-lines and watch the girl I love slip away from me again.

Tristan will forgive me eventually once he learns the truth, that I spent years pretending to just care about her like she was family, to appease her brother whilst he gave me his apologies each time his little sister had to tag along somewhere. In the earlier years when we were just kids ourselves, she could be a little annoying. But the older I got and as the years passed, she wasn't just a kid anymore and I found my-self wanting to be around her more, to protect her in a way that was more than just because she was Tristan's little sister.

It broke me when she left with little warning, though I don't think it would have made a difference either way. She kept it from me, like she'd made a de-cision to keep it from me. Had I done something to make her leave? No, surely not. I made it clear to her the day she left that if she ever needed me, I'd be there for her in an instant. The avoidance of eye contact and firm nod should have been indication enough that she clearly wasn't ever going to ask for help from me.

Well now she was going to get my help and be kept safe whether she wanted it or not, and to be honest I didn't know whether she felt the same as me, either way I'd be willing to spend the rest of my life convinc-ing her that I can be the man she needs.

Somehow, I manage to make it through dinner without popping a blood vessel, and once the table is cleared I make a swift exit to the back door and out into the garden. The cool autumn air does little to ease the anger I feel bubbling to the surface, all because of that waste of space she dated for almost two years, and anger toward myself knowing I was unable to help Grace when she needed someone. Anyone.

I'm outside cooling off for a few minutes when I hear the door shut behind me, and a moment later Tristan is standing beside me clearly trying to reel in the same anger issues as me. "What a fucking asshole. I need to make sure he goes nowhere near her". He turns himself to me so we are eye to eye now "Can you do me a background check on him? I need to know what kind of asshole I'm dealing with; I've only met him once before and I couldn't get a proper gauge on the guy". I snort at him. As if he thinks I didn't already do that.

"Tris, I checked him out when they got together. I have friends in Atlanta who did a background check for me and sadly the fucker came up clean". The look of shock on Tristan's face that I actually did that isn't lost on me, but he nods once, as if letting me know he approves of me basically stalking his fucking sister. "You know, I'm glad she has someone like you in her life, looking out for her and helping when she doesn't even realise she needs it sometimes". I turn away and grunt a response to him whilst looking out over the garden, trying not to give away too much that I'm actually still pining after the same sister he told me I could go nowhere near.

He disappears inside after a while, being called away by one of the kids and a minute later his spot is replaced by Grace. I smell her before I see her, inhaling her floral scent that she's worn since I can remember, and I turn my head slightly to take her in.

Her green eyes look much more vibrant when the sun is shining into them as she looks back up at me, doe eyed and a face full of questions. "C'mere" I say, as I reach my hand out and tug her into my side, wrapping my arms around her curvy frame. She stills for a moment before sighing and relaxing her body into mine as I lean down and press a kiss to the top of her head, inhaling her honeycomb shampoo. "It's all gonna be okay, you know. I'm here for you and so is your family, just let us help with anything you need Grace". She's quiet for a minute before speaking "Why are you being so nice to me? I thought you were angry with me when I left". I pull back to look at her, the confusion showing on my face. "Why in the hell would I ever be angry with you?" She pulls her gaze from me and licks her lips, as if trying to figure out what to say. "Well, you just seemed really upset with me when you found out I was leaving. I mean, I don't know what I'd done to piss you off, still don't know now".

I put my hand under her chin and pull her face up to look at me, god if only she knew. "Grace I could never be angry with you sweetheart, yeah I was upset you were leaving but who was I to stop you. I know you needed to do this for you". Her eyes flutter momentarily as she lets out the long breath she seems to have been holding for a while.

After what seems like forever, she finally brings her eyes to meet mine, her bottom lip pulled tight between her teeth. “I.. I needed a clean break from this life, this town. Everything just got too much for me here, so I decided to get a job away. It was all going well until the other night”. Blinking back tears in her eyes, she looks away from me again, but one slips free down her cheek and something snaps inside of me as I pull her back to me again.

“Fuck Grace don't cry baby girl, it's going to be fine. I've got you”. She grips me tighter for a minute, but just as I think I'm finally getting close to her, she pulls back quickly, flinching away from me like I burned her. Her eyes shift to the side to avoid me again as she wipes at the tears on her face “Erm sorry, I.. I just. It's been a long week and I.. I've got to get back inside.” She turns and walks back into the house that fast, she nearly trips on the step getting back in. Christ, I need her to be ok and not waste any more tears on that asshole.

My hands find my hips as I tip my head back, closing my eyes for a moment to try and focus on anything other than the way she looked just now. *Fuck I need to get out of here.* I give myself another minute before walking back inside to make my excuses that I have been called into work, so that I can get out of there and sort myself out.

After I've left the Vale's home, I decide I do actually need to distract myself for a while, so I head to the station to get some paperwork done and try to take my mind off everything for the evening. When I walk into the station, I'm greeted by a few of the guys, who seem to be having a discussion about the young girl they just checked in. I turn my attention to them, joining in their conversation.

"Seems to be a runaway that got herself into a little trouble, she's only fifteen so we need to contact social services." Mike, who is one of my sergeants, and the officer who checked her in seems to be dealing with the case. It seems like something I could use to get my mind off the day, so I suggest I take some of the case files to help out. "Alright, I've got some free time now, I'll take a look and see what we can do with her in the meantime". I take the file off him and head to my office, where I spend the next four hours trying and failing to get the memory of Grace out of my head that seems to be permanently burned in there.

By the time 8pm rolls around, I know I'm getting nothing productive done for the rest of the evening, and so I do the next best thing I can think of. Pulling out my phone I dial my second longest friend's number and suggest we head to the bar. He quickly agrees and twenty minutes later I'm arriving at our local… I'm not waiting long before I spot my friend Luca walk in and look around for me. His messy dark hair falls into his eyes, and he's dressed in his usual attire of shirt, jeans and boots. The bar isn't too busy and so he spots me quickly, making his way over to the booth I got us in the corner.

When he gets close enough, I get up to greet him with a quick hug and slap on the shoulder, before pushing his beer over to him that I got while I was waiting. "Fuck me" he says as he slumps down into his seat. "It's been a nightmare at the office this week. This is definitely needed today". He looks tired as he takes a sip of the cold beer.

Luca and I have known each other since middle school when he moved to Sweetwater. His dad decided he needed to be near family after his mom died, so he moved them here to be close to his aunt and grandparents. Along with Tristan, the three of us formed a bond and stayed close even through high school and college and it helped to have friends close when it was just me and mom after my dad died when I was just ten.

Mom didn't cope well with his death at first, so I spent a lot of time at Tristan's house. His mom and dad welcomed me with open arms and I felt like I became part of the family, whilst my mom left me alone a lot through my teenage years, preferring to spend her time with a bottle of wine to cover her depression.

But the Vales took me in and gave me the love of a family, and once Luca joined the two of us we were as thick as thieves, so to see my other best friend like this worries me a little. "You alright man? You look more stressed than usual. What's happening at the office?" Luca groans and drops his head back against the booth before going into his explanation. "We have this massive client at the office causing problem after problem. Feel like I can't catch a break". He picks up his beer and takes another sip before continuing "I honestly don't know why I thought it would be a good idea to join my dad's firm because it's gonna be the death of me for sure!"

Luca decided to go into architecture after leaving high school, following in his dads' footsteps. He's hoping to one day take over from him at the firm he started when they moved here. It's part of a bigger company and his dad's got offices all over the world, so it made sense for them to be closer to family when he was younger with his dad having to leave all the time. But now his dad gives him a hard time as he's brought himself into the limelight a lot more by being a bigger name at the company. He's clearly having a hard time with it right now, but eventually it should pay off. "Shit man, that's rough, has your dad had much involvement in it?"

He waves a hand in my direction whilst sipping his drink again. "Nah man, my dad said I need to step up if I want to take over so I'm having to deal with this on my own. The job will be completed soon, so long as the guy actually sticks to the goddamn plan, but anyway, are you all good? Not like you to call for a drink on a Sunday evening."

I sit watching the condensation drip down my glass, twisting it around on the table whilst I think about my answer for a minute. "Grace is back in town; I've been with the Vales for lunch and she was already there when I arrived. Apparently her dick of an ex decided it would be a good idea to cheat on her, she looked so lost today. I feel awful for her man". I spill my thoughts to Luca thinking he might actually be someone I can talk to, but when I look back up, he has a shit eating grin on his face, causing me to frown back at him, because what the fuck. "Why the fuck are you smiling like a dick when I just told you how upset she clearly was. Asshole". He shakes his head still smiling at me and shocks the shit out of me when he says "When are you gonna fucking admit you are in love with Grace Vale?" I feel myself stiffen and my palms go clammy at his statement. How the fuck does Luca even know? Fuck, what if Tristan knows?

I decide to play it cool, hoping he didn't notice my inner turmoil with a scoff and an eye roll. "How do you manage to come to the conclusion that I'm in love with Grace by saying she was upset? What the hell man". Luca chuckles and shakes his head at me *again.* "Please. You were obsessed with her when we were younger and she'd come out with us. Always checking in on her and picking her up if she ever needed a lift. Then when she left, you were always asking Tristan about her and moping round like a fucking sad sack instead of telling her how you felt. And to be honest I'd be surprised if Tristan didn't think the same" he says pointing his glass at me before taking a long drink from it.

Well, fuck. I mean he is right. If she was ever stuck I'd always offer to go and get her to save Tristan or his mom or dad from the stress of it and I thought I'd hidden it well but obviously I need to work on that, so I try to brush it off once more but I'm not sure I'm selling it. "We were younger then and she's like family, I like looking after her." I don't need other people knowing I'm in love with Grace before she does for god's sake.

I steer the conversation away from her and talk about work and Lucas' dad. He lets it go for now, but it makes me realise I need to speak to Grace. And soon.

5

Grace

After what felt like the worst weekend of my life, it was the start of a new week. Monday morning finally came around and I was going to spend the day trying to get my life back on track. Starting with a trip to the local cafe for my favourite, teacake and a vanilla latte. With it only being a short 15 minute walk into the centre of town from Rose and Hallie's house, I took the time to enjoy the changing of the leaves in the late September sun, and I'd slept awful the night before so I was up and out of the house early.

By the time I make it to the coffee shop, it's only just past nine in the morning and I just miss all of the school moms starting to descend on the café. It's a small hole in the wall, but the big open windows give it a bright and airy feel, with plants littering the place. After ordering my breakfast, I managed to snag a small table by the window so that I could enjoy the morning in peace, or so I thought.

"Grace is that you?" The town gossip is in the cafe bright and early, to get her fill of stirring her pot before the day has even hit noon. I suppress a groan and barely contain my eye roll as I square my shoulders and turn to face one my least favourite people for a conversation I'm clearly not going to avoid.

"Hey Alice, yep it's me". Alice claps her hands in front of her, a satisfied smile on her face while she gets herself ready for the line of question she's about to spew out "Oh I thought I spotted you coming from your parents yesterday, but I wasn't sure. Are you just here on a flying visit again?" I can't stand this woman, so trying to figure out how to get my next words out with my mouth without insulting her is quickly becoming a new talent for me. "Actually I am moving back to Sweetwater whilst I'm deciding where I'm going to move onto next."

Her lips turn into a sly smile, like she knows something that I don't. "Oh, are you and your boyfriend renting somewhere in town then? Your mom said you were happily settled in Atlanta". I try to keep my face as impassive as possible as I reel in the annoyance towards my mom. I knew this was coming and I love my mom, but why did she have to tell people my business.

Sitting up a little taller, I take a deep breath before giving Alice the information she is clearly digging for, because if she saw me yesterday, she clearly knew I was by myself. "No, actually. I decided I needed to come back home on a more permanent basis. Liam and I parted ways, so I'm here alone". Her hands come up to cover her mouth as if she's pretending to be shocked by my news, but we both know she doesn't give a shit but she wanted some of her gossip, so I threw her a bone.

"Oh gosh Grace, I'm sorry about that. How come you broke up?" I frown. Is this bitch seriously doing this much digging for gold today? But before I get a chance to tell her to take a hike, our conversation is interrupted... “Alice why don't you see if there is anything else the other women have to gossip about, instead of sticking your nose in where it clearly isn't wanted”. Both our heads shoot up to find the owner of the voice has stopped next to me, and I feel a little flutter in my stomach when I see Jaxx standing in his work uniform, looking about as annoyed as I am by Alice's line of questioning. He’s standing right beside me, his thick thigh so close it could brush against my arm, with his brow raised and arms folded like he’s waiting for her to move along.

“Oh Jaxx, I didn't see you there. I was just seeing if Grace was back in town for a while or not, it's just usually such a quick visit is all”. He lets out a small huff and slightly shakes his head at her. “From what I heard you were being nosey as per usual. Anyway, I need to talk to Grace, can you give us a minute?”

Alice scowls at Jaxx but doesn't say anything as she walks back over to her table and Jaxx takes a seat across from me, coffee in hand. “I didn't need saving from her, you know. I know how to handle her”. I mutter my annoyance to him. His lip tugs up slightly as he leans in and his gravelly voice vibrates through me when he murmurs back “I know you can, but she grates on me like you wouldn't believe, and I wanted her gone quickly”. I let out a choked laugh, I don't remember him like this.. One of the staff members brings over my teacake and coffee, breaking our moment. Taking a sip of my drink I look back up at him before asking “So, what did you need to speak to me about?”

He sits back a little, rubbing his hand over the back of his neck, a nervous tell of his "Oh, um... I actually wanted to see if you had plans tomorrow night. Thought you might like to go for dinner and catch up". I feel myself frowning at him, and he frowns back seeing my confusion. "You do know your Tristan's friend right? I know we're siblings and all but I'm not a substitute for when he's unavailable". Jaxx lets out a small laugh and shakes his head at me and it's not lost on me that he's finding this conversation amusing, "I know Grace. But I didn't miss your brother these past five years, I missed you. And since you avoided every event where I thought I'd get to see you again, if it's okay with you then I'd really like to take you to dinner tomorrow".

Well shit. I spent the last five years avoiding this guy like the plague and two days back in town he's already trying to spend time back in my life. "Jaxx.. I um.. I'm not sure that's such a good idea. I don't want anyone to see us and get the wrong idea. Hell, I don't want to get the wrong idea". I murmur the last part and I'm not sure if he actually catches it or not, but he sits forward a little, leaning into my space and smirks at me, his brow pulling up a touch before saying "And what idea might that be? We're just two friends catching up and sharing a meal."

He pauses for a minute, clearly not liking the way the conversation is going, and then shakes his head as if clearing his thoughts "Look if you don't want to then that's fine, I just would really like to take you to dinner and spend a little time with you, you've been gone five years, and that's a long time to not speak to someone, but I can see you're not interested so I'll just…." He starts to get up from the table and I panic. "No wait".

I pause, darting my tongue out to swipe at my bottom lip, watching him intently as he stops and looks down at me from where he is now standing, waiting patiently for my answer. "What time, and where?" He gives me his panty dropping grin that could make any woman swoon, then leans in to bring his lips to my ear and I let out a small shiver at the sensation of his breath tickling my skin "7pm, I'll pick you up." He presses a quick kiss to my temple before straightening, "Right, I need to head to the station, but I'll see you tomorrow Grace".

With a quick wink, he turns on his heel and is out of the door, giving me a view of that perfect ass again.

……

By the time I get out of the café it's almost 11am. I spent the entire time in my own head, trying to make sense of the situation with Jaxx. I make the short walk over to Rose's dad's firm to speak to him about the job he has going at his office. It's only a couple of blocks from the café, meaning I'm there in just under ten minutes as I look up to the building I could be working at. It's a brick building with lots of windows to allow light in, not like my old work that was dark and dingy.

Walking in, I instantly spot the receptionist, an older lady in her fifties, she gives me a warm smile as I approach the desk. “Good morning ma'am, how can I help you today?” I smile back at her. “Good morning, I'm here to see James Adler, please could you tell me if he is available”.

She quickly checks her screen before looking back up to me “He's just in a meeting at the moment, but he should be finishing up for lunch shortly. I'll give him a quick call to let him know you are here, may I take your name?”

“Oh yes, I'm Grace Vale, I'm a friend of his daughter Rose. He just said to pop in and didn't give a time, I’m sorry I should have called ahead”. She shakes her head but smiles back at me. “Not to worry dear, take a seat and he will be out with you shortly”.

I take a seat in the waiting area, trying not to fidget too much. It feels like I'm sat waiting for a life-time as the minutes tick by, but in reality, I'm actually only waiting ten minutes when James appears in the foyer to greet me. “Grace honey, it's really good to see you. It's been such a long time, how are you doing?” I shuffle my feet slightly, I don’t want to tell my friend's dad that my boyfriend cheated on me, that just sounds pathetic, so instead I opt for “I needed a change of scenery and where better to get that than back home”. I give him my brightest, most convincing smile I can muster up, and he seems to be convinced by it, as he puts an arm around my shoulder and turns me to walk toward his office.

He calls back to his receptionist to make us both a drink before opening the door to his room and showing me in. Once he's closed the door he invites me to take a seat on one of the comfy looking leather chairs, rounding his large oak desk to take a seat himself.

“So Grace, the job is basically for my head accounting role here at the firm. I know we are a small law firm, but the accounts can get very hectic. I need someone who can run alongside HR to do basics like paying salaries, but also someone who can manage all of the account’s finances for us. I’d like you to come on board as soon as possible to get to grips with everything before month end if we can manage that, and I will make sure to match your previous salary, with staff bonuses and perks of course. How does that sound to you?”

I look back at James with a slight frown tugging at my brow. “Oh, I thought this was an interview, not an actual job offer Mr. Adler”. He waves a hand at me with a smile, “Please call me James, and the interview is just formalities for HR but the job is yours if you would like it”. I sit back and think for a moment before deciding this is what I need. “Ok I would love to take the job; however I'm still working for my old company and will need to give notice. I hope that’s ok.”

He smiles back at me, seeming happy enough with my answer “That’s fine Grace, speak to your boss this afternoon and let me know a start date in the morning”. Wow this was not how I expected today to go. I smile back at James “Thank you so much for this opportunity, just from meeting your receptionist I already feel like I am going to enjoy it here”, he laughs a little to himself, “Oh yeah that’s Janet, she’s been here longer than most of the furniture so I'm sure you will both get on great”. We exchange numbers so that I can let him know once I’ve told Andy I'm leaving, and as I take my leave from his office, I say my goodbyes to him and Janet, and step outside to take a few deep breaths. This is good. I need this.

The walk back to the house doesn’t take long and makes me feel better than I have in days, maybe even weeks. I take in the scenery, sun shining on my face, the local park filled with young children playing and it makes me smile, I could definitely get used to this again. I send off a quick text to Rose letting her know her dad has offered me a job, with the promise of her favourite takeaway for tea as a thanks for sorting me out.

When I make it back home, it's just after 1pm, so I make myself some lunch and fire off a quick email explaining to Andy that I won’t be returning to the city and to accept my notice. He replies within an hour expressing how sorry he feels, but understanding the situation and wishes me best of luck, and thankfully there are enough people at the firm that he just takes my week away from work as notice, and once that’s sorted, I send over a message to James to say I'm able to start work from next Monday. He replies quickly and HR emails me the relevant documents I need to sign, and just like that I’m back to small town life

6

Grace

I'm Freaking out!! I got back home yesterday and told Rose and Hallie about Jaxx asking me out to dinner as *friends.* They both agreed with each other that I needed to look hot for tonight, and that is the exact reason why I'm currently wearing a hole into my bedroom carpet from pacing the floor. “Jesus Grace, will you just relax, he’s not going to jump you at the table.”

Rose and her sarcastic comment has me stopping in my tracks to glare at her. “Remind me why I'm friends with you again? I’m losing my shit here and you think this is funny. I feel too exposed in this outfit, it's just a casual dinner and he's going to take one look at me and bail”. I take another look at myself in the mirror and let out a groan.

Rose has dressed me in a satin top with a lacy trim that shows just a little too much cleavage, tight washed-out skinny jeans and a pair of strappy heels, and Hallie has gone all out on my hair and makeup. I usually only wear a little lip gloss and mascara, but tonight I have a full face and my hair is in big curls down my back. “I need to wipe this off, it's too much”. I say whilst frantically searching for my wipes. “What!!” Hallie pouts from where she is perched on my bed.

I look over to her letting out a sigh, “Fine, I’ll keep the rest of my face, but the red lip *has* to go”. “Ugh, don't be such a stick in the mud. You look hot!” Rose comments as she wiggles her brows at me but Hallie relents and stands to come over to me as she waves her hand in front of my face “Pass me the wipes, I don't trust you to not wipe your entire face off”, I glare at her too now, slapping the pack of wipes in her hand, she laughs a little at me, pulling a wipe out and getting to work removing the red stain from my lips.

I grab my lip balm and start applying it quickly to my now pink stained lips, when the doorbell goes. *Crap* he's early. Rose jumps up from the bed and is out the door of my room so fast I don’t have time to react, whilst Hallie laughs and comes back over to my side. “You look good Grace. Enjoy dressing up for a change”. I shake my head at her because I'm probably the least confident person out of the three of us, “What if it's just a casual dinner, like nowhere fancy and I'm super overdressed.” She smiles at me, winks and replies with “Then you will be the hottest woman there. Now scoot, I’ve got a date with a tub of Ben and Jerrys.”

She gives me a tap on my ass to shoo me out of the room, following me downstairs to where Rose is chewing Jaxx's ear off about her new brownie recipe she’s trying out this weekend.

As I reach the bottom step, I look up just in time to catch Jaxx looking me up and down, mouth slightly open. He's wearing a simple blue button down, black jeans and Timberlands, with a tan jacket pulled over the top. He looks *hot.* “I'm overdressed aren't I. It’s

Rose's fault, she dressed me. I.. I'll just go change." I turn to run back up the stairs and change, but before I get anywhere Jaxx replies to me. "Absolutely not Grace, we're going somewhere nice, and you look perfect. Grab your coat and we'll get going, it's cold out tonight."

Rose gives me a sly smile as she passes me my trench coat and leans into whisper in my ear. "Maybe he will jump you at the table after all". When she pulls back, she gives me a wink and I give her my dirtiest look in return. She just laughs at me and pushes me toward a waiting Jaxx.

"You kids have fun tonight and don't bring her home too early now Jaxx". He laughs at her bad joke as he takes my hand, tugging me closer to him and murmuring "Wouldn't dream of it" then shoots me a wink before turning and leading me out to the car, where he opens my door for me before rounding the other side to jump in. It's a nice car, nothing flashy or brand new, like Liam always wanted, the cool leather seats hit my back, sending goose bumps up my spine.

We're only driving about 5 minutes, listening to a country station playing in the background when curiosity gets the best of me. "So where are we going then if it's somewhere nice". I need to know every detail possible so that there's no surprises. "Patience, Grace. You'll find out when we get there, it's about a thirty-minute drive if that helps you". I roll my eyes dramatically at him, making him chuckle in return. "It doesn't but thank you very much" I huff out a breath, fold my arms and sit back trying to figure out where we are going but it's no use, I hardly remember anywhere around here anymore, and I realise how much has changed as we drive along the road.

The old church that once sat almost wreck and ruin has had some sort of modifications done to it, and a few new houses have gone up along the main road out of town. I feel like I have so much to figure out again here, starting with the man sitting next to me.

I turn to my side slightly, trying not to be obvious whilst I'm watching him drive. His brown hair is smoothed back, beard freshly trimmed like he's just been to the barbers, and that gorgeous earthy scent of his which fills the car and fogs my brain slightly, but I'm a sucker for punishment, so I inhale it whilst trying and failing not to get too wrapped up in my own head over how tonight is going to go.. "I can see you watching me, you know. Stop being a little creep and talk to me."

I snort out a laugh at my failure to keep my perving to myself. "I just feel odd, like I'm going out with my brother's best friend for dinner, does that not seem like an odd thing for you?" I rush the words out as I ramble, and Jaxx stiffens slightly but quickly recovers with a shrug of his shoulders. "I missed you a lot when you were gone, I think you forget how close we actually were, and then you left without saying a proper goodbye Grace. I won't lie, I was gutted, but I know you needed it, and just hoped you would eventually come back".

His answer leaves me feeling even more confused than before about this whole evening, so I push forward. "But I was just Tristan's little sister, I really didn't think you would be *that* bothered by me leaving". He turns to look at me, brow furrowed like he's not sure he should say what he's about to come out with, but he does anyway.

"I've thought of you as more than his little sister for a long time now, and I just thought I'd have more time with you, but then you told me you were moving, and I didn't want you to stay here for me. You needed to live your life, and I wasn't going to hold you back, so I kept my feelings to myself and let you go".

I'm speechless. How do I even get my head around that? He's had feelings for me this whole time and I left because I couldn't bear to see him with anyone that wasn't me. I feel like I'm having an internal meltdown and I let out a sad laugh, close my eyes and put my head back against the seat. "What's wrong Grace? Talk to me" he asks from across the seat, a worried tone in his voice. After the longest minute I turn my head to face him, give him a wry smile and reach for his hand on the centre console.

"All these years I've been almost hiding from you, because I thought you just saw me as the little sister, and I didn't want to torture myself anymore knowing I couldn't have you". He blinks back at me, eyes going wide like a deer caught in headlights. After a moment, what I said must fully register because he bursts out laughing.

"Well, that certainly changes how I thought this evening was going to go". He shakes his head trying to stop the laugh that won't seem to stop before continuing "I had this whole speech in my head to try and convince you that we would be a good idea together, but knowing what you just said makes things a lot easier". I freeze momentarily, because part of me wants to be happy that he feels the same way, but the irritating part of me stupidly thinks about my brother. "What about Tristan though? He'll lose his shit if he finds out". Jaxx glances over to me, unimpressed by my reaction to him. "First of all, it's when your brother finds out, not if. And secondly, leave your brother to me. We're grown adults and this isn't some fling I'm proposing, I'm not a dick Grace. He knows I wouldn't treat you like shit like…" He stops himself before he can finish his sentence.

I finish the sentence for him though "Like Liam you mean? I was stupid not to see what he was doing under my nose the whole time". I puff out a long breath before continuing, "He probably didn't treat me right for a while, I was too wrapped up in my own head convinced I needed to make things work that I let the little things slide. He'd always be working late or being called into the office on the weekends. Probably was to see her, and I didn't even realise until it was too late".

Jaxx clenches his jaw, whilst his hand grips mine a little tighter. "I will never treat you like that asshole. I can't promise I won't mess up the odd time, no one is perfect. But I'll try my hardest to show you I'm the man you deserve, I mean it Grace" I squeeze his hand back, just as I realise my favourite restaurant is coming into view, my frown instantly changing to pure excitement. "Stop it. You did not book my favourite restaurant. How the hell did you know?" He smiles back at me as he pulls the car into park, reaches over and grabs my chin to turn me towards him. "Do you remember your eighteenth birthday? You were fuming because your mom and dad forgot to book a meal because they were too busy helping your sister. She was just about to give birth to Brody and was being as demanding as ever.. I asked Tristan where your favourite restaurant was, and he told me here. So, I booked it for us all and told him to tell you it was him. I wanted you to have a good birthday". He gives me the sweetest smile and I feel my heart pound in my chest. Fuck, he's literally been doing this shit for years, and now he's gone and booked the most amazing Italian restaurant.

I beam back at him, giving him my brightest smile. "Thank you so much for telling me that, it was one of the best birthday's I've had". He gives my chin a little squeeze before releasing me and climbing out of his door. "Wait there", he says as he rounds the car and is opening my door for me, taking my hand in his to help me out.

He leads me to the restaurant, hand in mine and I'm smiling like a friggin' idiot, trying to wrap my head around how I went from dreading this evening, to it quickly becoming one of the best yet. Once we're inside and the maître d' has taken our coats, we are led to a booth in the back where we slide in and Jaxx takes up space right next to me. The restaurant is gorgeous, dim lighting throughout, and each table is far enough away so that each party can have their own intimate conversations, whilst white tablecloths and pillar candles with a small vase of roses next to them decorate each table, I'm starting to realise it's a lot more romantic than I remember when I was eighteen.

Jaxx is so close right now, that he'd be able to hear my heart pounding from the excitement of this evening. The waiter comes over to take our drinks order, and once we have given our order and the waiter has left us, Jaxx turns to face me, a semi-serious expression marking his features. “I meant what I said in the car Grace. I want you and have done for a long time. And I'm pretty sure your little confession in the car tells me you want me too, want this between us”. He wiggles his fingers gesturing between the two of us.

“Do you know when I realised that I had some sort of feelings for you Jaxx?” I peek up at him as I ask, and he shakes his head a little, so I continue, “I was seventeen and had snuck out to a party with Hallie and Rose, and had gotten wayyy too drunk to properly function”.

He clenches his jaw again, giving me a firm nod urging me to continue. “I called you crying and asked you to come get me, and you came and got me even though it ruined your evening. You looked so angry at me but promised not to tell anyone the state I was in, and then you held me and told me everything would be okay, and I believed it. I knew I could trust you with my life and I'd be safe.”

He looks me dead in the eyes, a slight curve to his lip and gives me a reply that sends tingles up my spine. “I knew you were at that party, Grace. A friend of mine was there and called to let me know, he knew you were Tristan's sister and underage, and I asked him to make sure you were safe. I was waiting in my car a block away when you called because there was no way in hell I was letting you get yourself home. I've always got you, and I'm watching out for you even if you don't realise it. I'll always come for you baby girl".

Heat pools at my core at his admission, and my panties must be soaked, because *fuck*, I'm so hot for this guy right now, after he just admitted he basically stalked me to make sure I didn't get into trouble. Jaxx moves a little closer to me and I feel myself shiver from the heat of his proximity. He leans in to speak next to my ear, his husky voice deep and low "You've always been mine, even when you didn't know it. And now, now I have you and I don't plan on letting you go".

I pull back slightly to look at him, and the fucker is smirking at me, so I smirk back. "Well Jaxx, you might think you have me, but you'll have to chase me first". His deep laugh vibrates through him, and he turns to look at me, steely grey eyes shining with mischief.

"Well baby girl you better run then. Because when I catch you, I won't ever let you go".

7

Jaxx

Fuck me.

The things I could do to this woman sitting in front of me. I need to remember that she's just gotten out of a relationship though, and not push anything too far with her. I've waited far too long for this moment to finally arrive where we both know how we feel about each other. But what she's just said, makes me think that maybe she wants to take things slowly, so I do what I'm good at and ignore the little voice in my brain telling me that I need to behave.

I run my hand up and down her thigh just to be able to feel that she's real and actually here with me, and I watch as her thick thighs pinch together like she's trying to stop herself enjoying the moment. She sucks in a sharp breath, making a little gasping sound as I continue the torment not only for her but for myself too. I look up to see her sparkling green eyes assessing me, a small frown tugging at her beautiful face, her bottom lip is tucked into her mouth and I just want to pull it out and bite it myself. I suppress the groan which is bubbling up my throat, while my dick instantly hardens at the thought of her pouty lips pressed against mine.

I sit watching her for a minute trying to figure out what she's thinking because if we weren't in a restaurant full of people, I'd fuck her at the table right now. I still can't believe she was going to change when I arrived, I don't know why because she looks fucking stunning.

She doesn't normally wear a lot of makeup but tonight she's wearing a full face. It's not too much though and makes her features stand out more. She's wearing her eye makeup a little heavier too, and it just makes her big green doe eyes sparkle even more than they already do. Her outfit is simple but shows off her curves beautifully, with her top just a little on the bustier side giving me the perfect view of the ample cleavage, that's going to be just the right handful when I finally get my hands on her. Christ, I sound like a fucking teenager, and if I don't reel it in, this night will be ending a lot sooner than I hope, and not for good reasons either. My hand comes up to brush against her cheek, tucking a loose strand of hair behind her ear as I go. She shivers a little at the movement, and I need to know what she thinks about this crazy little revelation of ours. "Talk to me Grace, what's going on in that beautiful head of yours?" Her tongue darts out and swipes across her bottom lip as she lifts a hand to run it through her hair. She looks like she's stuck on what to say in case she'll upset me, but I'd wait a lifetime for this girl, and nothing short of her saying she's leaving me again could do that.

Her eyes dart to the side momentarily, the tablecloth seemingly the most interesting thing in the room right now. I watch as the cogs turn in her head as she tries to put her words together "I…. I just want to take things slow with us for a little while if that's okay, especially since I just got out of a relationship, and I need to make sure we're doing the right thing here. All I keep thinking is how pissed off Tristan will be if he finds out". She lets out a small, defeated sigh like this isn't a problem we can fix.

I need to talk to my best friend as soon as I can to eliminate that problem for her, he'll get over it eventually if he is upset with me, but I really fucking hope he isn't. I take her hand in mine, the other gently tugging her chin to face me again. "Like I said before, leave your brother to me, I'll handle him. And we can go as slow as you like, I'm not here to rush you into anything you aren't comfortable with, so let's just take things one day at a time". She seems to visibly relax into me a little more after reassuring her, giving me a little smile so I know she's ok for now.

A short while later the waiter comes to bring us our drinks and takes our food order as we settle into a comfortable conversation about our jobs and life over the past five years. "I got offered a job at Rose's dad's law firm yesterday. It's still in the accounts department and a little more work than I usually have, but I've said I'm going to take the job. I think it will be good for me, I can't work remotely for my old company forever so this will definitely help me if I'm going to stay here permanently".

She seems excited about her starting up her new job, I reach across to her squeezing her hand, "That's awesome Grace, I'm proud of you" and I am proud of her, because her getting a job here means she's not planning on going back to that fucker, and staying for the long run, which I know she won't admit, but she's scared of the commitment that comes with that. If she did ever decide she wanted to move again, I could always get a transfer, but that's hopefully something that's way in the future that we don't need to worry about right now, *and you're getting way too carried away*. I ignore my inner thoughts and fill her in on some of the local town news and new places that have opened that she might be interested in, and by the time food comes she seems to have relaxed a little more than she was when the night begun, digging into her pasta and letting out little moans whilst she enjoys her food, but my dick clearly thinks those little moans are for him as I get impossibly hard again and I have to try and subtly adjust my jeans without her noticing.

By the time we make it back to her place it's almost midnight. We got so carried away in conversation, that the staff were almost having to ask us to leave so that they could close. I pull onto her drive and put the car in park, before hopping out and rounding to her side to get her door. She giggles as I take her hand and says, "You know, I have been opening my own car door for a while now, you don't need to get it for me". I tug her up and closer to me, my lips tilting up into a smile. "I know you can get it, but I'm here and I can do it for you. So let me, please".

I lift her hand in mine pressing a kiss to the top of it and when my eyes reach hers again, she's smiling back at me, and I feel my heart rate pick up the pace with that look she's giving me. I walk her to her door and as she puts the key in she turns to me, "Thank you for such a lovely evening Jaxx. I haven't enjoyed myself like that in a long time".

I lean into her and snake my arm around her waist as I pull her close to me, lifting my other hand to tuck a stray hair behind her ear. "This is just the beginning of many evenings you'll enjoy when you're with me baby girl."

Stroking my hand along her jaw, I pull her face slightly towards mine, giving her a chance to back out if she wants me to stop, but she doesn't. Her breathing gets heavier and her eyes dart between mine, looking for the same confirmation as I am. Her tongue swipes out across her lips as she gives her head the slightest nod to give me the go ahead, and I don't waste a minute as I press my lips firmly onto her plush full ones.

My hand slides to the back of her head whilst my other grips her waist a little tighter causing her to let out a little moan, opening her mouth just enough for me to push my tongue inside. She lets me take over the kiss as my tongue explores her mouth whilst I feel her delicate hands grabbing onto the back of my jacket. When she finally pulls back, her eyes are dilated and her breathing choppy, her lips a little swollen too and I smile back at her disorientated look as she bites her bottom lip. Pulling her close to me again and murmuring in her ear "I'll be seeing you very soon baby girl".

When I finally pull back away from her again, she hovers a little by the door before going inside, but not before giving me a small wave. "Looking forward to it, night Jaxx". I get just a glimpse of her sultry smile before she closes the door, and I'm left standing like a fucking idiot smiling to myself at the door.

I get back into my car and have to sit for a minute whilst I come back to earth. I feel like I'm wide awake right now, with the buzz from the evening still keeping me going. I drive around for a little bit, knowing I won't get to sleep anytime soon, my mind going over everything we talked about. By the time I fall into bed, sleep evades me for the rest of the night as I spend it tossing and turning, my mind going over how I didn't pull my head out of my ass years ago and get the girl sooner.

8

Grace

Liam: I fucked up and I want to make things right. Please can you come home so we can talk about things and work this out. I miss you. xxx

Jaxx: Had a great time last night, I've already got our next date up my sleeve ;) x

I wake up to both texts and let out a sigh as I look at my phone, trying to decide if I want to even bother giving this absolute tool a response. I decide against it for now, and reply to Jaxx instead.

Me: Me too! That sounds promising, I'm looking forward to it. :) x

Jaxx: Are you free on Sunday? I have the day off. x

Me: I'm sure I can free up my diary for you. x

Jaxx: Perfect see you at 10am Sunday. I'll pick you up again, wear something casual.. Although if you want to save those heels again for later I won't be complaining. x

Me: I'll make sure to keep them nearby. ;) See you then. X

I throw my phone down onto the bed, my head falls back into my pillow with a smile on my face. I don't want to get too carried away with Jaxx, but I've wanted this for so long and I actually thought at one point that this was never going to happen. My mind drifts to Liam as I flit between deciding if I was really in love with him, or if it was just the idea of him and I was just comfortable with the situation.

The more I think about it I am definitely coming to the realisation that it wasn't a love relationship and more just a friendship by the end.

I stay in bed for five more minutes before deciding I should get up, and eventually drag myself into the shower to get ready for the day, running over what I'm going to say to Liam in my head. I only want to message him once and be done with it. Whatever I say needs to be the right words so that he gets the picture.

Once I've washed my hair and finished putting makeup on, I check my phone again to see my sister has messaged asking to meet for breakfast. I fire off a quick reply and finish getting ready.

About thirty minutes later, I'm walking into the café for the second time this week and spot my sister with Max in the corner. He reaches for me when I get to the table, and I pluck him out of her hands, taking a seat across from her as she pushes my favourite coffee and a teacake across to me.

She doesn't wait long before jumping into her motherly badgering though, “How are you feeling now you've had a chance to settle in?”

I look up to see Lily's got a worried expression on her face, her brows knitted together and green eyes the same as mine searching my face for any hint that I'm not actually ok like I'm about to say I am. “I'm fine Lily, I’ve been doing a lot of thinking, and to be honest, I don’t think I'm as upset as I feel like I should be about the situation”, shrugging my shoulder, I continue, “It’s been a big lesson for me to be more careful who I let in to my life, but at the same time, I’ve come to realise I don’t think I was actually in love with Liam. He just fitted into my life and made it more comfortable. We weren’t romantic like we should have been, hell we only had sex once a month, twice if I was lucky, and I'm realising now that he just didn't do it for me, not like I want”. *Not like Jaxx,* I think to myself, but I don’t say that to her.

She gives me a firm nod and a small smile in return. “That’s good then, so long as you're ok, but please, if you're not doing ok then tell someone. None of us want you to be down or upset, we all just want the best for you”.

I reach across the table and give her hand a quick squeeze, “I know, and thank you, everyone has been so good so far and Ja….” I stop myself quickly hoping she didn’t just hear his name come out of my mouth, but she has the hearing of a bat and her brows shoot to her hairline in surprise to my mention of him.

“What about Jaxx, Grace? I thought we didn't talk about him anymore?”

She smirks at me knowing full well I was obsessed with him when we were younger and when I left town, I told her I didn't want to hear about him anymore. “He.. We.. Well, he took me out to dinner last night. Said it was as friends for a catch up, and it might have turned into him admitting he’s had feelings for me for a while”. I feel myself go beet red at my admission and when I look up to my sister, she’s grinning like a fucking Cheshire cat. I roll my eyes at her, “Stop looking at me like that, I told him I wanted to go slow with things. Tristan will kill him and I'm terrified to tell him”.

Lily scoffs and waves her hand around in my general direction, “Tristan will be fine and I'm pretty sure he knew something was going on between the two of you years ago, just no-one said anything to anyone by the sounds of it”. That has me raising my brows right back at her, mouth gaping open. She reaches over and pushes my jaw closed, laughing at me. “Sitting catching flies isn't a good look sis”.

I shake my head to clear my thoughts, “But he *always* said his friends were off limits to me, and I'm off limits to his friends”, the confusion in my thoughts laces my voice, “Well I guess Jaxx is the exception to the rule then”. She shrugs a shoulder and continues, “Jaxx is a good guy, the whole family has known him almost his whole life, he's basically one of us. Just something to think about when you're taking things *slow”*.

Max uses that moment to start wriggling about on me and starts fussing, so Lily takes him back from me to feed him whilst changing the subject on to mom and dad arguing about her wanting to buy sheep. I keep trying to pay attention but I'm distracted for the rest of breakfast, because now all I'm thinking about is kicking things up a notch with Jaxx.

Once leaving the café having had breakfast with my sister, I wander around the shops trying to see if I can find some outfits for my new job when my phone pings.. pulling it out I groan out loud at the name on my screen.

***Liam*:** You can't ignore me forever Grace. We need to sort things and you need to answer me. I'll call you later.

Not with that attitude I won't, fucker. Deciding to ignore him some more, I slide my phone back into my pocket and go back to shopping.

A couple of hours later, and a few bags in hand I head to a nearby place to grab a late lunch, and I'm sitting reading through the menu when Jaxx steps up beside me looking godly and beautiful as always in his police uniform. His cream shirt is fitted lovely and snug over his toned arms, and his work trousers are just the right amount of tight. I slowly bring my gaze back up to his face not hiding that I'm checking him out and he smirks back down at me. "Enjoying yourself there Grace?" I sit back a little, cross my arms over my front and slide him a quick once over again before giving him a firm nod. “Yup, the view is pretty spectacular from where I'm sitting”.

He chuckles at my comment, and I gesture for him to take a seat across from me. “Are you just stopping by or do you have time to join me for lunch?” He looks at his watch quickly but nods and takes a seat. “I can spare half an hour for you”. I clap my hands together and say “Oh lucky me, hopefully the town gossip doesn't spot us and think I'm in trouble with you technically being on duty”. I shoot him a wink making him laugh at me.

“I think the town gossip would be more intrigued as to why I'm spending my time alone with a stunning woman”. I blush at his comment but frown at the same time. “What do you mean they would be wondering that, I’m sure you spend plenty of time with attractive women”.

He looks back at me and raises a brow as if that would totally never happen. I roll my eyes at his reaction “Ugh, please, you’re telling me you don't ever spend time with other women”. It comes out as more of a statement, but my question has him looking serious again. “I dated people for a little while after you left but I haven't seen anyone in about six months”. My eyes bug out of my head as my brain works to figure out how the hell this beautiful human has managed to go so long without female company.

He must see the question in my eyes and continues, “I spent a lot of time wondering.. No, hoping you would come back. And after about a year I made the decision to at least try and see other people. I struggled to find anyone to settle down with, so after my last relationship ran its natural course, I decided to just stay single for a while. Good job I did really, or we wouldn't be here right now, would we?”

I'm about to respond when my phone starts ringing on the table. Jaxx and I both look down to it and see Liam’s name across my screen. Jaxx frowns at the screen as I breathe out a sigh, sending the call to voicemail. “Is he bothering you?” I look up to see him still frowning at my phone and the last thing I want is secrets between us, so I decide to just come out with the truth. “He messaged this morning saying he had fucked up and wanted me to go back to Atlanta so we could talk”. Jaxx’s gaze meets mine again, anger simmering in his eyes “No fucking way are you going to meet with him. After what he did to you, he can go fuck himself”.

He sits back and folds his arms across his chest, a childlike action but it has his muscles flexing under his shirt, and I find my gaze dropping to his arms. *Focus Grace.* I clear my throat to refocus my thoughts, but his stance has me getting defensive. “I know Jaxx.” I hiss, a little too angrily “I haven't responded to him, that’s why he’s calling me. I’ve been trying to figure out what to say to him so that he leaves me alone for good”. He huffs out a breath and nods to the phone. “Then tell him you are with me now and to kindly fuck off”. I let out a laugh shaking my head. “I think that would just piss him off more”. He smirks at me, clearly relaxing a little knowing I'm not going to go running back to my ex. “Good, the way he treated you he deserves to feel like shit”.

I know I need to message Liam soon and make it very clear to him that we are never getting back together, because now all I want for the rest of my life, is the man sitting across from me.

.....

By the time I get home from what turned into an hour-long lunch with Jaxx it's almost 4pm. Rose has just gotten in from work and gets excited when she comes into my room and spots all the bags in my hands. "If you had said you were going shopping, I would have cleared my day". She's barely actually paying attention to me as she pulls every item out of the bag to examine it. "Eh it's okay, I ran into Jaxx and had lunch with him, so I wasn't a total loner all day". She stops short and looks up to me. "Wait, you and Jaxx went for lunch.. Today… When the two of you went for dinner last night?"

Spinning herself around she plops down onto my bed, crossing her legs and leaning back on her hands. "Spill", she wiggles her brows at me as she waits for an explanation, and I huff out a long breath walking over to sit on the chair across the room, "Yeah, we went for dinner and things ended up taking an unexpected turn. He told me he has feelings for me and wants us to start seeing each other".

Her eyebrows shoot to her hairline, and she lets out a low whistle "Oh hell, I wasn't expecting that. Are you going to start seeing him? I know you've technically just gotten out of a relationship, but the guy was a tool. Sorry but we all could see it, we just had to let you get there on your own".

I think about what she's saying for a minute and give her a slow nod. "I think I want to give things a real try, I'm just concerned about how my brother will take it. It's his best friend, and I don't want to come between them, Jaxx has said he's going to speak to him and it will be fine… and I believe him. But you know as well as I do that I've pretty much been in love with Jaxx since I hit puberty. I thought I would have grown out of it but all my feelings came flooding back when I saw him at my parents place the other day".

She nods at me, a smile creeping up on her lips as she mulls over my answer. "Then what is there to think about? You both like each other a lot, and you're both consenting adults. I only see it going well if you ask me, you've bagged the town hottie that everyone wants but no one got". Letting my head fall back against the chair and looking up to the ceiling I mull over her words for a moment before deciding to tell her about Liam.

"Liam messaged me this morning too, saying he fucked up and wants to talk. He then decided to ring when I wasn't responding to him, and Jaxx saw him calling. He wasn't happy, but what was I supposed to do.. I need him to leave me alone and I don't want to get into a texting war with him, but I do need to send him a message to let him know it's not going to happen. What should I say to him?"

Rose pats the bed next to her for me to join, and I get my phone out to start a new message. We go through what to say to him, and after about twenty minutes of writing, deleting and re-writing the message, I'm happy enough with it to send it to him. I re-read it one last time before hitting send.

Me: Liam, I'll say this once and once only. Get it into your head that we are never getting back together. What you did to me is unforgivable and has made me realise that we weren't actually that good together anyway. I wish you no harm for the future, but you need to leave me alone now. I left my key to the apartment and have taken everything I might need. You need to get on with your life and let me get on with mine.

I send him the text and take a deep breath, knowing that I'm doing the right thing. But less than five minutes passes when my phone pings again.

Liam: No, you don't get to do this to me. I will prove to you that I am the person you should be with. I love you, and I know you love me too. I won't stop until you are back here where you belong, with me.

Me: You're actually more delusional than I thought if you think we can work through this. Leave me alone and don't contact me again.

He sends me another string of messages, but I delete them without reading what he has to say. I need to just put it to bed now and carry on like he didn't exist. If only it were that easy.

9

Jaxx

Finishing time tonight can't come quick enough. I've got a massive case load on my desk, and I feel like it's just a never-ending pit at the moment. My eyes begin to ache from all the straining I'm doing to them, and I feel a headache coming on, but it's not even 2pm yet and I let out a groan because I feel like sticking pins in my eyes.

Mike decides to choose that moment to knock on my office door pulling me from my thoughts, "Got a moment? I've got some more info on that young girl we pulled in the other night". He steps into my room, and I gesture for him to take a seat on the other side of my desk, he passes the papers over to me as he takes a seat. "What did you find out?" I ask scanning through her file. "She seems to have come from absolutely nowhere. We can't find any documents for her. It looks like she doesn't exist but she's not talking. I've tried getting social services involved but they are taking forever to get back to me and asked us to hold her until someone can get to us".

"Fuck sake" I mutter whilst trying to figure out what more info we can find.

"I'll get in touch with a couple of my detective connections and see if we can pull any info from other countries for her. She might have come over under a false name." He nods to me as I hand the papers back to him, and I ask him about his wife, "How's Jenny getting on with juggling the kids now she's gone back to work?" He huffs out a laugh shaking his head a little, "She's driving me fucking nuts. I think I preferred her not working to be honest", I nod along "Yeah I can imagine her being busy with the kids is a full-time job in itself". He nods back at me, "Don't I know it", we move the subject along to the kids and that his oldest got onto the baseball team at school and as we're chatting my phone lights up on my desk, and I smile down at it seeing Grace's name on my screen. "Who's got you smiling like a lovesick puppy?" I look at him and he's grinning at me like an idiot, his face matching my own. "You'll find out soon enough" I reply to him as I grab my phone off the desk. But when I open the message my smile quickly disappears..

Grace: I'm guessing the flowers are from you? If so, thank you xx

"Oh, not so lovers in paradise then?" Mike says grimacing at my face a little and I look up to him frowning, because who the fuck is sending my girl flowers that's not me. "Someone's sent the woman I'm seeing flowers, and she thinks they're from me. But I have a pretty fucking good guess who sent them". Mike takes that opportunity to leave as he jumps up and starts heading out the door. "You call her, I'm gonna go look into this kid some more". I wave my hand in his direction, "Alright I'll catch you in a bit".

Scrubbing my hand over my face I press call on Grace's contact info. She answers on the second ring, blissfully unaware she's got the wrong attention. "Good afternoon Jaxx, I have to say I'm pleasantly surprised by this.". I stifle a groan and hope she's not too upset by the outcome. "They're.. Grace they aren't from me. I didn't send them". "Oh…" That's it. Silence. "Grace… Did you speak to Liam?" I try to keep my anger in check at the thought of that fucker trying to win her back. "Um, yeah I messaged him on Wednesday after I saw you, but I told him it was over and not to contact me again.. Do… Do you think these are from him? Urgh I should've fucking known, he knows I hate roses". She's quiet for a moment before continuing, "He doesn't know where I've gone, and I've not told him anything so I just don't get how he might have found where I am, I don't even think he's ever even been to this house". I rack my brain trying to think how he may have known that she was there. "Did you tell anyone from your old town where you were going?"

I start typing away at my laptop trying to pull some things together from the info I got on him a while back. She's quiet for a moment, presumably thinking who she could have told. "I only told Andy, my old boss, about the situation. He's like a second dad to me and I was emailing him back and forth the past couple of days. I did send him my forwarding details for work, and my new address."

Just as she's telling me what she can think of, the info pops up for Liam on my screen. "Does he still do IT work Grace?" My eyes scan the screen "Erm, yeah from what I know. He never talked about work to me, so I couldn't be one hundred percent sure". I sit staring at the screen for a minute trying to figure out if this guy could actually be so desperate to hack into her accounts, but the odds are looking likely. "Grace, sweetheart. You're going to have to make a new email. I think he's hacked yours and has been reading what you have been sending to people."

She lets out a little gasp over the phone "Oh fuck, are you kidding me? That absolute dick". Her almost yelling down the phone causes me to pull it away from my ear a little "Grace, stop, just take a breath. It's fine we can fix this, just make a new email and then he won't know what it is to access it. Was there a card with the flowers?"

I feel like I'm on pins waiting for her to search through them, "Mmm.. Oh shit yeah there is, I didn't even see this when they came". She's quiet for another moment whilst she opens the card, then lets out a sigh over the phone. "What does the card say Grace?" I feel like I'm grinding my teeth to the bone from the amount of tension going through me right now. "It says, miss you, I'll see you soon.. Yup it's got to be from him. Fuck.. I can't believe he's fucking tracked me down".

I feel the panic surge through me, knowing that he's taken to sending her shit when she's asked him to leave her alone. I'd go and arrest the fucker if I could, but you can't exactly arrest someone when you don't have sufficient evidence, so I settle for, "Just throw them away if you don't want them. Take a picture and keep the note though, I feel like he's just getting started". "Okay, will do". We chat for a little while longer and when she hangs up the phone,

I get straight to work calling Harris, a guy I met and became friends with through some work colleagues. He became a private detective a little while back, and he's come in very handy when I need info fast.

"Jaxx, nice to hear from you, although I'm guessing this isn't a social call". His friendly voice filters through the phone and I grunt in response. "No, unfortunately I need you to look into someone for me please. He's a friend's ex-partner, and we are pretty certain that he's hacked into her emails to find her address. I need some up to date info on him if you can get me anything?"

I hear rustling in the background, as if he is looking for something. "Go ahead, what info have you got on him so far." This will be an easy trace for him, "You've actually looked him up before for me. Liam Fennel. 28, works in IT the last we know of." He's quiet for a moment whilst he must be trying to remember who he is. "Ah, yeah I remember the guy, nothing major came up on him though".

My head falls back into the chair, as I stare up to the ceiling and let out a groan "Yeah well, I'm starting to think something might come up on him now. If nothing comes up then I don't need to worry, but I'd rather be safe than sorry".

"Sure thing Jaxx, anything else you need?" I let him know about the young girl we have held in the cell, and to look her up too. We end up having a small catch up over the phone before ending the call.

By the time I'm done with work my head is pounding, but I feel like I need to do something to release some of this frustration from the day. I head out for a run hoping that will sort me out and do about 3 miles ending up near Grace's house. I'm tempted to stop in to check on her, but I think better of it, knowing she'd probably find it weird me showing up on her doorstep at 9pm. Instead, I do what I know I should and head home; as I'm running back I think of what I can do to cheer her up.

10

Grace

After the unwelcome flower delivery from Liam, I did as Jaxx asked and took a picture of them and the card, before promptly throwing them in the trash. Annoyingly though, I then spent the rest of the night worrying about whether he will actually come looking for me here. But after a restless sleep and a deep need for coffee, I'm grinning like an idiot when I come downstairs and find a fresh set of sunflowers sitting on the kitchen counter with a vanilla latte and a card taped to it.

To make your day as bright as these flowers are.
Enjoy your coffee.

Jaxx

X

Hallie is sitting on the sofa looking through the news channels, she peeks her head over the sofa to where I'm standing, “Don't feel too special, he got us all a cup. He had to run to work though so I took them off his hands". She holds up her own coffee cup shooting me a wink, and I stick my tongue out at her as I make my way over to the sofa to join her.

"He's so sweet, can't say I've had a guy do that for me". I smile into my cup at her comment, but then quickly remember why he would have sent me them. "Ugh, he's trying to make me feel better. Liam sent me flowers and a creepy note yesterday, I never even told him where I was moving to and Jaxx seems to think he's hacked my emails". Hallie winces a little "Rose filled me in on your message conversation with him the other day, what a weirdo. Don't worry girl, we can look after you".

"Why are we looking after her? Ohh coffee. Thank the heavens". Rose rambles as she comes into view looking a little worse for wear, hair sticking in every direction and the remnants of last night's makeup on her face. She grabs the last coffee cup from the side and takes an instant sip. "Ahhh, so good on a hangover." Hallie and I laugh at the absolute state of her and then I fill her in.

"So after the little text conversation me and Liam had the other day.. He didn't quite take the hint like I thought he would, and sent me roses yesterday, those" I say pointing to the new bouquet on the side, "Are off Jaxx to cheer me up, and the coffee is from him too!" I hold my cup in the air showing her ours too.

She comes into the living room and plops herself down onto the loveseat, taking another sip of coffee whilst in full thought. "That man is an absolute godsend, bringing coffee and flowers on a Saturday morning to cheer you up". Hallie butts in grinning, "Yep and he didn't forget about the other two important people in her life".

Rose sighs happily. "Girl, get me one of him". "Amen" Hallie says next to me whilst raising her cup making us all burst into laughter at our little trio. "Right, Rose, you better sort yourself out before tonight. Grace here promised me a night out and I am holding her to it, so you are coming too". *Damn* I forgot all about that. "Urgh," Rose groans. "I'm not sure if I have the energy for this, I'm getting too old". Hallie scoffs at her "Please, you're barely twenty-six and you're acting like you're forty. Drink your coffee, go back to bed for a little while and be prepared to have the night of your life".

With that she jumps up from the couch. "Right, I'll see you both later, I'm off to join my new running club again", and with a wink she spins on her heel and is out of the door. "She's definitely getting some from one of them". Rose says, smirking into her cup. "I hope so" I reply, looking out of the front window to where Hallie is talking to one of the runners. "At least she's having fun".

With a final nosey at her new friends, I get up from the sofa. "Ok, I'm going to get a long shower, then start trying to find an outfit for tonight, you should probably catch an hour extra of sleep too, and a shower because I can smell the wine on you from here".

I wave my hand in front of my nose, laughing when Rose grabs the cushion from behind her and launches it at my head. "Don't worry Grace, I can look hot as fuck when I need to. Don't let this fool you" She calls from behind me as I head up to get a long hot shower.

....

Feeling thoroughly cleaned and having shaved every inch of my body for tonight and put a mask in my hair, I take a look at myself in the mirror and spot the dark circles under my eyes from a restless night's sleep. Knowing I'm not out until later on tonight, I put a face mask on and sit reading my book for a while.

I must have fallen back asleep because 2 hours later, I'm woken by loud music blasting from Rose's room. I get up and take my now dry face mask off, before making my way into her room, to see her dancing round the bedroom to 90's pop music in nothing but a towel and singing into her hairbrush. I snap a quick picture of her thinking I'll save that for a birthday post, and luckily she doesn't catch me as she spins around and spots me watching her.

She just gives me her brightest grin and carries on jumping about, and when the songs finished she finally turns the volume down, arms in the air posing like she's just finished a routine. “See, good as new and I'm a little excited for our night out now”. I laugh at her craziness and take a seat on her bed. “Hallie will be home soon but we need to decide what we are wearing tonight. I'm thinking you should wear something sexy” she says pointing at me and I frown back at her. “What's wrong with jeans and a nice top? There's nothing wrong with what I wear”.

Rose smiles back at me, her expression letting me know I'm clearly not wearing what I want to this evening as she proceeds to walk out of her room and into mine. I groan at how annoying she can be but follow her into my room where she is pulling everything out of my wardrobe and throwing it at me to try on. She spins on me, giving me a pointed look with her brow raised as she twirls her finger at my feet, “You're wearing heels tonight too. No questions”.

Looking down at my feet I wiggle my toes, wondering if I have time to get a pedicure, Rose must read my mind because that’s the next thing out of her mouth. “Get dressed, I need to go into town and you need to sort those piggy’s out.” I scoff at her, a small smile tugging at my lips “You’re so rude sometimes. I don’t actually know why I stay friends with you”. She eyes me mischievously and gives me a shit eating grin “I’m not rude, I'm honest and I want you to look good, so throw something on and I'll meet you downstairs in ten”.

Twenty minutes later than we were supposed to, we are finally getting into the car to head into town. Rose is driving and looks over to me in the passenger seat before focusing back on the road, “I booked us both in at my usual salon and they have space to do nails too if you like. Thought you could use a pamper day, my treat”. “Sounds amazing to me since you just said you’re paying”, I reply grinning at her, and she shakes her head.

A few hours later I feel like I've been fully pampered. I decided to go for matching hands and toes in my favourite nail colour, a deep emerald green, knowing I'll be wearing something black tonight so they will go. Once leaving the salon, we head across the road to grab some coffee, and then pop into a couple of shops before heading back to get ready for the evening.

....

By the time we are all dressed and make it to the nicest bar in town, the place is already heaving. We flash our ID's to the doorman and make our way inside and straight to the bar, where Hallie flags down the bartender and orders us all a cocktail to get us started, whilst Rose looks for a table and I scan the place. It's an old building, which has been done up, but keeping the older features, low hanging globe lights are spread along the vaulted ceilings, none of the chairs match, and the walls are pulled back to bare brick giving it a rustic feel.

We eventually spot a booth in the corner and start making our way over to it, but a group of guys beat us to it, we give each other an annoyed look and are about to turn and look for somewhere else to sit when Hallie appears beside us. One of the guys in the booth waves at her to come over, and it's then I recognise them from outside the house this morning. “These are the guys I go running with, looks like they have space at their table, if you two are okay with it we can join them”.

Rose and I give our nod of approval, take our drinks from her and follow her to her new group of friends for the evening. “Girls, this is Matty, George and Josh. These are my best friends, Rose and Grace”. We say our hellos and all squeeze into the booth together where Rose and I are next to each other and Hallie has taken up space next to who I think is Matty. He's tall and blonde like her, with a little stubble and is leaning into her ear to talk to her, and she's giggling at whatever he is saying.

This must be the reason she likes running so much. Rose throws herself straight into conversation with George and I am left feeling awkward and unbelievably sober next to Josh as he leans in to speak to me, I can tell he's half gone already by the way he’s talking. “You're really pretty you know”. I laugh awkwardly because I don't usually have guys hitting on me, and this one’s not helping with the way he's slightly slurring his words.

I need to get more alcohol down me before I can even tolerate sitting listening to this. “Uh, thanks. Where’s your girlfriend tonight?” I ask because I'm hoping he keeps the conversation less flirty, and I feel like I'm such an awkward person when speaking to new people. “Oh baby, I'm very single, and I'm thinking you are too”. When he gives me a drunken smile I grimace slightly, I mean he’s good looking but I'm absolutely not looking for anyone now I know me and Jaxx are on good ground.

“Oh sorry, but I'm taken”. At that he lets out a little laugh and shakes his head. “Damn why do I always get the unavailable ones. That’s a shame, because you are stunning in that little black dress". His hand strokes up my leg a little as his eyes roam over my body like he can see what's under my dress and I try to stay polite and smile back at him because I'm that kinda girl, but all I want to do right now is get away from this guy, I nudge Rose and pull her from her conversation by whispering into her ear. "I feel really awkward having a conversation here, can we go dance?"

Rose turns her body slightly to look him over and nods to me. "Excuse me but me and my friend are gonna go dance, could you let us out" she shouts over to him and a slow smile creeps up his face as he moves out of the booth to let us past, but barely giving us enough space. As I'm standing to squeeze past him, his hand grazes my ass and I swear he squeezes a little. If I wasn't sober, I probably wouldn't have noticed, but I am so I shoot him a dirty look as I drag Rose to the dancefloor.

We make our way into the middle of the crowd and find a little gap to hover for a while, and I lean in to speak to her "Thank you for that, he's giving me the creeps a little. Told him I'm unavailable and he doesn't seem to care". She shakes her head looking annoyed. I'll get George to switch with him and you can sit next to me when we get back to the table".

I nod in agreement, and we continue dancing. After a little while Matty brings us over some fresh drinks from the bar and then carries on to the table where the other guys are sat, and with a little wave over to her, Hallie comes to join us after downing some more of her drink and we spend the next few songs dancing away.

My feet are killing by the time we sit back at the table, where the group finally settle into nice conversation and I've all but forgotten about Josh and his wandering hands as the night wears on, but after a while I'm starting to feel a little tipsy, so I decide to go and stand outside for a little while to cool off and get some fresh air. Letting the girls know where I'm going, I slip out of the booth and head to the door, my mind in another world as I grab my phone out of my bag to text Jaxx.

11

Jaxx

I fucking hate working Saturday evenings.

All it ever seems to consist of is dealing with idiots who can't hold their drink, and they end up wandering into traffic or causing a problem. Tonight is no better. It's 11pm and the new hot spot in town is already crawling with idiots, and since we have nothing better to do on our Saturday, we decide to park up to keep an eye on them. I know Grace is there with her friends tonight, so at least this way I can keep an eye out for her without it looking like I'm being creepy, as well as doing my job. I'm working the shift with Mike, who is sat engrossed in something on his phone whilst I take over lookout, we tend to do this every time we work the late shift, taking it in turns half an hour at a time and then we swap over, keeping the rotation going for the evening.

People are milling about outside the bar, and I get a flash of ebony hair I'd know anywhere, stepping out into the warm September evening. She's wandering along the sidewalk not paying any attention to where she is going and has her head in her phone typing something out on it, swaying slightly as she goes, and I quickly realise she's a little tipsy.

She comes to a wobbly stop, smiling down into her phone whilst tapping away, my phone pings and when I look down, I see her name lit up on the screen, and I know she’s got a grin like that because she's actually messaging me. It's drunken gibberish, and I'm typing out a reply to her when I look up and see a guy she seems to know approach her. I feel a little jealousy going through me, but I tamp it down just as quickly, because I trust her and she’s just talking to someone she knows.

Except when I look closer, she’s shaking her head at him and backing away slightly, my eyes instinctively flit over to where the door staff are a little further down hoping they will notice her, but they are dealing with a drunk guy passed out on the floor, and everyone is watching them meaning no one but me notices what’s going on.

I give Mike a nudge and I’m about to tell him I'm going over to make sure she's alright, when I see the guy grab her and start pushing her backwards into the nearby alleyway. “Fuck” I shout, which has Mike’s head shooting up. “He's.. Shit! I need to go help her, follow me”. I’ve barely got my words out before I'm swinging the door open and running down the road to where Grace has disappeared. Mike’s talking into his radio calling for backup whilst trying to keep up with me, and by the time I’m halfway across the street I feel like the air has been sucked out of me as I frantically race to get to her, whilst I'm getting more panicked by the minute knowing she's not safe.

I’m right near the entrance to the alley when I hear her muffled screaming not too far away, and I'm instantly on high alert, picking up the pace to get to her faster. By the time I reach the alley it only takes a second to spot her, where the guy has her pinned up against the wall with his leg spreading hers, and his body holding her down. He's got one of his hands over her mouth, whilst trying to get his other up her dress.

She's crying and shaking her head, and all I see is red. Flying down the alley I'm at her side in a second and Mike and I have to use a little force to drag the guy off her. Without even thinking, I shove him against the opposite wall and throw a punch to his face, connecting with his jaw, watching as his head rolls about.

It's then that Mike grabs me and shakes his head, "You deal with her, I've got him". He's nodding in Grace's direction, and when I turn to her she's slid down the wall to the floor and is shaking and sobbing uncontrollably. Her makeup is now streaked down her face, and her hair that was slick down her back only a few minutes ago is now roughed up and all over the place. The strap on her dress is torn slightly, exposing her shoulder to me, goose bumps running down her pale arms and legs.

I steel myself as I try to be as calm as possible around her so as not to scare her anymore, but as I crouch down to her level and reach for her, she pulls away from me, her crying gets worse as she shakes her head rapidly whilst trying to crawl away. It's killing me seeing her like this, but I know I need to be strong for her. I do what needs to be done at that moment and grab hold of her by the arm a little firmer. I pull her into me, cradling the back of her head against my chest where my heart is beating frantically. "Shh Grace, it's ok. You're ok. I've got you sweetheart" I say as I try to soothe her, rubbing circles across her back, and she must recognise my voice because she instantly freezes, it takes her a moment but eventually she pulls her head back slightly to get a look at me.

I give her a tight smile as she searches my eyes with her own terrified ones, tears staining her beautiful face and I nod to her whilst trying to comfort her some more, my hands come up to rub up and down her arms, keeping the chill off her whilst also trying to bring her back to the here and now. "You're safe now sweet-heart. He's not going to hurt you."

With that a sob lurches from her throat and I pull her back into me. I hold her for a minute before putting my arm around her back and the other under her legs, and once I know she's secure I lift her into my arms, keeping her shielded from seeing the guy who's just attacked her as Mike hauls him away into the car.

We stay in the alley for a moment as I try to let her calm down by herself, the sobs that come from her shake her entire body as she wails a little more into my shirt, staining it with her mascara, "Shh, sweetheart, it's okay, please don't cry. I've got you now, you're safe", I repeat the words to myself more than her, but it helps to stop her crying nonetheless, and when we eventually walk back out of the alleyway I spot another police car that has arrived. It takes a minute to cross the road, where a small crowd has begun to form outside the bar from nosey drunk people. I keep her face hidden as best as I can, so no one sees that it's her, she'd hate to have to face questions from people she barely knows in the coming days. When we make it to the second car one of the officers opens the door for me and I try to put her down in the back seat, but she's grabbing a hold of me tightly, her arms are like a vice around my neck.

I decide it's probably easier to just slide into the car with her at this point, and I struggle a little putting us both in, but once she's seated, I pull her face back so it's level with mine. "Grace sweetheart, I need you to stay in the car for a minute whilst I speak to the other officers. Are Rose and Hallie still inside?" She nods to me, still in a daze from the night's events, so I take her phone that she's still clutching and send a text off to Rose saying briefly what's happened and that I'll take her home with me.

Turning to Grace, I give her one more squeeze as I press a kiss to her forehead, "I'll be back in a minute, I'm not leaving you tonight". Her tear-stained eyes stare back at me, she's shaking and trying her hardest not to start crying again, but a tear breaks free and slides down her cheek. I wipe it away with my thumb before pressing my lips to her head for one last kiss, and climb out of the car.

As I walk over to the other car where that piece of shit is being held, I take a good look at him. He's no older than thirty, with shoulder length, dirty blonde hair. He looks well put together, but the look in his eyes makes me think he's taken something. "Have you drug and alcohol tested him? It's quite obvious he's drunk but I'm wondering if he's taken anything else with the way he's just been".

We both turn back to him, and he's now slumped in his seat falling asleep, "Nah, but I will do it when we get back to the station and I'll make sure all the paperwork is sorted. I'm guessing that's the mysterious woman you wouldn't tell me about. By the way you were just speaking to and holding her it seems like you care about her a lot" he says, hiking his thumb over his shoulder towards the car Grace is in.

I rub my hand over the back of my neck and let out a sigh, "Yeah that's Grace, she's Tristan's sister so I better call him and let him know what's happened, but I might wait until the morning now, since it's" I look down to my watch, "Fuck, it's 12:30am. You better head back to the station so that you can get signed out. I'm going to get one of the guys to come with you and the other to drop us back at my place. I don't want to leave her alone tonight and her friends are still out, I told them I'd take care of her and not to worry".

He nods along agreeing with what I'm saying, "No problem, you just get her back and I'll sort the rest out". I give him a solid tap on the shoulder in thanks, he's a good guy, and seems to help me more than the others do. I say my goodbyes to Mike as he rounds the car to the other side and jumps in whilst waiting for the other officer to join.

When I make it back to the car, Grace is curled up on the back seat seeming to have calmed down a little, I speak to the officer outside for a moment, giving him my address, and we climb in the car where I pull her into me and settle into my seat, but as soon as she realises I'm back her arm shoots out and grabs me around the waist. I put my arm around her, pressing a kiss to the top of her head.

"We'll go to my place if that's ok. I don't want you to be alone and I don't have a key to get into yours.

Are you okay with that?" She just nods her response, and I let the officer in front we can go.

12

Jaxx

Grace is so still and quiet by the time we get to my house that I figure she's fallen asleep. It's short lived though when I go to pull her out of the car, because she starts thrashing and screaming at me to get off her. I reach for her again and she pulls back so hard she almost smacks her head, she'd clearly been having some sort of nightmare, so I grab a hold of her firmly trying to still her. “Grace, Grace!” I say firmly to her, causing her to go still, her green eyes darting up to mine, still slightly wet with tears from the night. “You’re ok sweetheart, we've just arrived at my house. We'll get you in and settled, if you just come with me”.

She’s still not speaking properly but turns her head to get a look at where we are. Eventually she looks back at me and bobs her head once, then begins to climb out of the car. I take her hand trying to steady her but her heels are doing us no favours right now so I lean down and sweep her up into my arms. She lets out a little squeal, but quickly wraps her arms around my neck whilst I carry her in. Turning my head slightly, I give my thanks to the officer who brought us home before turning to walk up the steps to my front door.

Once we get inside, I take her straight over to the couch and place her down on it, kneeling down to take her shoes off. I look back up at her, watching as she tries to come back around from the evening's events. I'm not sure how much she had to drink but I'm hoping it's not so much that she can't keep anything else down. Tapping her on the leg to get her attention, I speak as gently as I can, trying not to scare her any more than she already is tonight "Wait there and I'll grab you a glass of water". I climb to my feet and leave her for a moment to go into the kitchen, grabbing a glass from the cupboard and heading over to the fridge for some cold water. I take a minute to myself, resting my head against the fridge, as I take in the night's events, my head is swimming with all kinds of thoughts and I'm just thankful that I got to her in time. What would have happened if I didn't spot her? No one would have seen.

I shake the thought off and head back into the other room, and by the time I get back to her, she's much more alert and her head spins in my direction when she hears me. I hold up a glass of water and some Tylenol I grabbed off the side on the way in and place it in her hand. "Here take these they will help, and drink all of the water". I watch her as she looks around for another few seconds clearly deciding if she's safe here, and when she seems to come to the right conclusion in her head, she sits back slightly into the sofa.

Looking up to me, eyes lined with unshed tears she finally speaks, "Thank you for this, helping me. I'm so lucky, and thankful that you were there", her voice wobbles slightly but she continues, "I don't know what I would have done if he..” she can't get the rest of her words out as she chokes up a little, and I'm down on the sofa with her in an instant pulling her into me, “Hey, hey, look it's ok. I got to you in time and you're safe. I know it's hard but try to take your mind off it”. I pull back from her slightly to get a look at her and she nods to me. “I need to go set the spare room up for you, are you ok here for a minute?” I want her close to me right now, but I'm not sure if she’s comfortable sharing a bed with me tonight given what’s just happened.

Her eyes widen in panic though, and she shakes her head slightly at me, her eyes darting to the floor to avoid giving me eye contact. She's picking imaginary lint off of her dress as she asks, “Would it be ok if you stayed with me in the same room?” She's so quiet that I barely hear her, but I catch enough, and relief floods through me that she wants me close, but I still want to make sure I'm not pushing her boundaries any further than she wants. Putting my hand under her chin I lift her head up to me so that I can look her in the eyes.

“Of course I will, I can sleep on the floor and you take the bed..” she's shaking her head quickly again and that has me shutting up, “I don't want you sleeping on the floor, I’ll share your bed with you, if that’s ok that is.” Her eyes shift away from me once more, as her tongue darts out and swipes across her lips.

She looks so beautiful right now, and it's taking everything in me not to drag her up to bed this minute, but she’s been through a lot tonight and the last thing I want is to take advantage of her. “Yes Grace, and if it wasn't for the circumstances, you know I'd always be more than happy to share a bed with you. C'mon let's get out of these clothes and I'll find you something to wear to bed”.

I stand from the sofa and take her hand in mine, leading her upstairs and through my room into the bathroom. I leave her standing at the door whilst I look for a spare toothbrush and washcloth and once I find it I place them on the side before turning to her. “Here you go. There's soap there to wash your makeup off and these to brush your teeth”. She nods to me, and I step out of the bathroom whilst she gets sorted.

Making my way over to my drawers I dig out an old t-shirt and a pair of sweats she can sleep in and put them on the floor near the door, knocking to let her know they’re outside as I go into my wardrobe to change into something similar for bed. I normally sleep naked, but I feel like she wouldn't appreciate that right now.

After a few minutes I hear the bathroom door click open and she steps out in just my t-shirt. The sight of her has all the blood rushing to my dick making me curse myself, because *fuck* she looks so good, fresh faced and with just my t-shirt on, creamy skin and toned legs peaking out from under the hem of *my* shirt.

She clears her throat, and my eyes come up to roam over her face before giving her body another scan over. Her bottom lip is tucked between her teeth, and she’s got her hands in front of her, wringing them whilst she looks around the room for a moment before saying “The sweats were too big so I'll have to sleep like this. Um, which side do you normally sleep on?” I have no words because my brain has forgotten how to function right now, but it keeps going enough for me to respond by nodding to the left side, she looks at it for a second before she rounds the bed to the right and climbs in.

I stand there, rubbing the back of my neck and not knowing what to do for the first time in my life, and she giggles at me. “You can get in bed, you know. I don't bite”. *No, but I might.* An exhausted laugh slips out of me as I look at the ceiling, before bringing my face back down to meet hers. “No but, I don't want you to feel uncomfortable after..” She's shaking her head at me and holds her hand up, causing me to stop mid-sentence. “You are probably the best person for me to be near right now, so please don’t make it weird and get in the bed”.

I eventually relent and climb into bed, turning off the lamp and getting comfy, but I need to be closer to her, and so I pull her towards me bringing one arm around her, and making lazy circles along her arm with my fingers whilst her head rests on my chest, she settles into me straight away, and I know I've made the right decision to bring her here tonight. After a minute or two I give in and tell her what’s on my mind, hoping she's still awake. “I wish what happened tonight wasn't to you, and I can't help but feel some sort of guilt that I couldn't get to you sooner”.

She's still for a moment and I almost think she’s fallen asleep until her head turns slightly, and she peeks up at me from under her thick dark lashes. A small frown appears in the crease of her head as she props herself up on me to start her little scolding session. "Jaxx don't you dare blame yourself for that jackass doing what he did tonight, it's my own fault for not being careful and aware of my surroundings. But you.. you saved me, and if it wasn't for you god knows what would have happened to me". She shudders and closes her eyes to take a deep breath.

My hand comes up to cup her face and I stroke the back of it along her cheek "All I ever want is to protect you. I could have killed that guy tonight for touching what's not his, but you are my priority, and you always will be". Her eyelids flutter a little as she whispers to me "Jaxx" she's so quiet I almost miss it, but I most definitely don't miss the next words that leave her beautiful lips, "Kiss me. Make me forget". *Fuck me.*

I have to every ounce of my restraint so I don't throw her on her back right now, but I lean in closer, brushing my lips against hers. Our lips touching gently for just for a moment before drawing her closer, deepening the kiss, and pressing more firmly against those soft plump lips. I get a taste of minty breath just as a little moan leaves her mouth, allowing me entrance. I take the invite she's giving, pushing my tongue in and swirling it against hers, my hand coming up to cradle the back of her head. My dick takes over the kiss instead of my brain, and I can't help myself as a groan slips out of my mouth causing her to whimper back a little in response.

My brain, taking a little longer than it should, finally kicks in as I pull back slightly, she follows me forward a little before stopping, her eyes shooting open and searching mine trying to figure out why I pulled away, and I'm lying there trying to figure out the same thing. '*cus your meant to be taking it slow tonight, fucking idiot.*

The disappointment shows on her face as she bites her lower lip and I feel my dick harden more at the sight, forcing myself to swallow the groan that's trying to surface. She tries to pull away from me, thinking I don't want her, so I grip hold of her just that little bit more, holding her in place. "As much as I want to carry on Grace, and trust me I do, it's been a heavy night and I don't want to do anything you'll regret in the morning. I've waited a long time to have you, and I'm not about to have the first time I fuck you be tonight of all nights".

Letting out a breathy laugh she tips her head up to look at me, trying to hide that she's upset we aren't taking things further, and fuck, the sight of her with messed up hair and big green doe eyes staring back at me makes me want her in the worst way possible. I roll us, moving over her so that she's lying on her back, and lift myself up and onto my hands allowing me to hover above her. Raising my brow, I give her a pointed look and she looks away shyly, clearly thinking I don't want her as badly as I do, her eyes are swimming with worry and regret, but not because she wished she hadn't started. "I'm sorry I got carried away, I just need you close, I want to be close but I'm starting to feel like maybe you don't want that too", she breathes out the words with shaky breath as I bring my hand up to her face, dragging it back to facing me and lean in close, my lips barely grazing hers.

“If you want to come baby girl, then just ask. I can make you feel good and forget, but I'm not fucking you tonight”.

Her eyes widen slightly as she goes to pull away from me, but I hold her in place, “Use your words and give me an answer, and I’ll give you what I know you want”. She nods slowly at me but it's not enough, I need to hear her say it. “Words Grace”.

“Yes”.

13

Grace

"Yes what, Grace?"

I'm squirming under him a little, his gaze is so intense on me, and he's trying to get me to tell him that I want him to make me come. Words are failing me right now but in my head all I'm screaming is *YES, YES, YES!*

I wriggle under him a little more, but it just causes him to press his hips into me, and any thought I had that he wasn't interested in this is thrown right out of the window, because *shit.* Jaxx is hard as a fucking rock above me and those sweats he's wearing are doing little to hide it.

My legs are on either side of him and I'm pretty certain those fresh grey sweats are going to be ruined momentarily because I'm so wet right now, and the little lace thong I have on is doing very little to protect me from anything right now.

He lets out a low groan that almost sounds like a growl as he leans back into me. "Tell me what you want Grace, and I'll help you out". He presses himself into me a bit more and I let out a little moan, and his head drops down to my face a little more as he releases a throaty laugh. "Baby, I'm a patient man and I can wait all night long, but I know you don't want that, so tell me I can touch you".

I finally find my voice, but it's barely above a whisper as I give him the permission he's waiting for. "Touch me Jaxx, please". His fingers move down my throat, trailing lightly across my collarbone, and down to my breast to give it a squeeze over my shirt. "You want me to touch you here?" "Yes" I pant out, but he's not finished.

His fingers skim over my sensitive nipple causing it to harden and pebble beneath the cotton shirt, and he leans in to kiss the base of my neck, sucking slightly on the sensitive flesh there. Once he's satisfied it's enough, he moves back away from me again, carrying on his tortuous journey down my body by dragging his hand over my ribs and down to my hip bone. When he gets to the base of my t-shirt which has risen up my legs, he slides his hands under it and splays his fingers over my stomach.

"What about here, Grace? You want me to touch you here?" I nod in response because I don't trust my mouth right now, but it's not enough for him as he grips the side of my hip, his long fingers digging into the flesh there. "Word's baby, or I'll stop right now".

Fuck. I squirm a little more before huffing out a breath. "More, I need more", it comes out more like a moan rather than actual functional words, but it's enough for Jaxx as his hand carries on it's journey again, moving at a lazy pace, his fingers run across my lacy underwear and down to where his fingers meet my overly heated core, and he rubs his thumb firmly along my slit, pushing my underwear up into me and causing friction.

My eyes close and I let out a small cry as I hiss out the words “Ahh yesss. Please, more. Please”. My hips shoot up involuntarily into his as his mouth comes down on mine hard, rushed, desperate. His thumb is still rubbing over my underwear, and my body automatically grinds into him, before he suddenly pulls back and removes his hand. My eyes shoot open as I look up to see him grinning down at me. “That’s more like it, baby girl. I'll give you what you want, but I'm damn well going to take my time with you and enjoy this”.

He sits back on his heels, gripping both of my hips and toying with the string on the side of my underwear. “Well, these aren't much use are they? You're fucking soaking Grace, and I've barely even touched you yet”.

I feel the heat creep up my face turning me the darkest shade of red as a wave of newfound shyness takes over my body, making me feel like I need to hide myself from his piercing gaze, but as I try to pull my shirt further down my body his big hand reaches out and grabs my wrist, stopping me. “I didn't say you could move, did I?” I shake my head at him, which is rewarded with a satisfied smile. “Then be a good girl and keep your hands at your sides and do not touch yourself unless I say so. Understand?” I nod at him, but he shakes his head and tuts at me, “Words Grace”. “Ahh, um. Yes, I understand”.

Pulling me up into a sitting position, his fingers toy with the hem of my shirt again “Arms up baby”. I do as he says and he pulls my shirt over my head. I find myself holding my breath as his eyes roam appreciatively over my body. “Fuck Grace, you're absolutely perfect” he continues with his appreciation for another few seconds, before using his hand to push me back down gently and comes to lean back over me, dipping his head to put his mouth over my breast, licking at first in lazy circles with his tongue before giving it a little suck and then nipping it with his teeth, making me let out a small yelp.

He lets out a small chuckle as he moves his attention to my other one, doing the same to that whilst one of his hands comes up to cup the first, his fingers playing with my nipple, rolling it between his fingers and I let out a moan as he pinches it a little tighter, “Baby, these were made for me. The perfect size to fit my hand and mouth around”.

With one last little nip, he pulls his mouth away and his lips come back to mine, grazing my lips with his teeth.

My breathing is heavy, and my lids are partly closed but I feel his presence all over me, his musky scent taking a hold of my senses and giving me brain fog. But I'm still trying to focus on him as his lips move down to my throat, nipping back at the sensitive flesh on my neck, while his hand moves down my body again before he pulls back abruptly, grabs either side of my panties and rips them down my legs, tearing them slightly.

I instantly frown at him, “They were fucking expensive”. He laughs at me as he moves closer “They were getting in my way. I’ll buy you more”. The small hint of anger I had is instantly gone, and replaced with tingles all over my body as his hand lightly strokes over my slit, dipping in slightly to spread my wetness all over me.

“Fuck Grace, baby. You're so wet. Is this all for me?” I remember my voice this time whilst nodding enthusiastically at him “Yes” I moan as my hips move of their own accord trying to get friction from him, but its short lived when I let out a sharp gasp as he firmly presses his thumb against my clit whilst sliding a finger inside me, right up to his knuckle. “Ahh, Fuck”. My hips buck and I'm breathing heavier now, his breathing matching my own but he's clearly holding himself back. His finger moves in and out before he adds a second, stretching me as he goes at a slow and torturous pace, and he finally begins moving his thumb in circles over my extremely sensitive clit. “Is this what you want? You want to come”.

He's asking me but it doesn't come out as a question, as he begins to increase his pace, his fingers begin moving faster as I feel my insides start to tighten and my body heats with need, bringing me closer to the edge. I'm so close and in my own world feeling like this is some out of body experience, that I don't expect him to suddenly stop and pull back. My eyes open and I’m instantly up and leaning on my elbows. “What the fuck Jaxx! Why did you stop?”

His steely grey eyes burn into me, and a sexy smile creeps up his face making me wonder what’s coming next “You think I'm going to let you come and not taste it for myself. Lie back baby, let me taste you”.

Embarrassment takes over me again as I feel my face start burning for a second time tonight, he must sense my hesitation as his face instantly changes to worry. “What’s wrong Grace? Talk to me”. I look away from him, embarrassed that I actually have to admit this to him. “No one has.. done that to me before”. He goes white as a sheet, but I see the wheels turning into his head as he comes to the wrong conclusion. “Grace. You’re not… You've had sex, right?”

That redness I was feeling creep up my face has taken over my whole body now as I go a deep shade of crimson, nodding quickly and trying to avoid his gaze as his body visibly relaxes. “Yeah, I've had sex. Just not had anyone go down on me before, it's just never happened”. He hangs his head and shakes it before looking back up to me, a newfound hunger in his eyes as his lips tip back up into a smirk. “Well then, I guess I'm the lucky bastard that gets to have the first taste. Now lie back baby, let me enjoy this because I fucking know you will too”.

My head drops back against the pillow as Jaxx brings his body down closer to mine. He starts again, kissing between my breasts then slowly trails his lips back down over my body, before settling in, with his head between my legs. He uses his elbows to push my knees farther out and open me up to him, and I can't help but look back down to see him looking at me and licking his lips like he’s about to have the best fucking meal of his life.

His hands come up to either side of my inner thighs slowly making their way to the tops of my legs, before he uses his fingers to hold me open, taking one long lick up my core. "Ahh" I moan, but he's just getting started.

He uses his tongue to make small circles over the sensitive little bundle of nerves pressing firmer as he swipes across my clit. I wriggle a little under him and my hips try to buck up, but he holds me back down with one large hand covering my lower stomach, the other he uses to slide two fingers inside me, rubbing them against my walls which brings the building sensation back with full force.

His teeth graze over me as they bite at the slightly sensitive flesh, before he licks and sucks again bringing me closer to my climax. Pulling his face away from me I get his sexy as fuck grin as he licks his lips before saying, "This is the best pussy I've ever tasted, and it's all fucking mine". I'm too overcome with the heat building inside me to respond as he bites down on my clit again, pushing his fingers further inside and making me squeal.

"Do you hear me Grace? You're mine, this is mine. I've waited too long to have you, and now I've had a taste. I'm not letting you go".

His words have me coming undone, and I cry out his name as my orgasm takes over my body and my legs shake uncontrollably, while my head thrashes about. He carries on pumping his fingers inside me as I come back down from my high, feeling a little lightheaded and completely spent from the best orgasm I think I've ever had. After a few minutes my brain still isn't working properly as I feel Jaxx lean over me, and I come back round a little more as I'm pulled up into a sitting position and he taps my thighs, "Arms up baby".

I do as he says, and he pulls the t-shirt back over my head, pulling the covers over the two of us and pulling me back into him.

One arm is tucked under me and the other wrapped tightly around my waist, as he brings his lips to my ear and speaks lowly, “Next time, when I take you, I won’t be so gentle”. I shiver at the touch of his lips tickling against my ear, and he nips at my lobe before kissing the top of my head “Sleep sweetheart. I'm right here”.

I snuggle down into him and quickly fall into possibly the best sleep of my life

14

Grace

I'm woken by the smell of coffee on Sunday morning. It filters upstairs and mixes with what smells like bacon and makes my stomach rumble, but I ignore the feeling and try to keep my eyes closed for a minute longer as I take in the smell of the sheets.

It smells like Jaxx, and I feel myself smiling into my pillow remembering what he did to me last night, how he made me feel. And now I'm bright red at how embarrassing I was, because I'd never had oral. *Jesus.* He was just so good with me though, excited even at the thought he got to do that first.

Rolling over to my side I check the clock on the bedside table, 9am. I let out a groan as I roll back into my pillow, before deciding I should probably see where Jaxx is, throwing the covers back as I pull my legs to the side of the bed beside and giving my body a good stretch.

After ducking into the bathroom to do my business, I make my way downstairs and follow the smell into the kitchen where Jaxx is standing at the stove in just a pair of shorts, hair wet like he's just gotten out of the shower.

He must hear me approaching because he turns to me grinning, with his perfect straight white teeth on display, coffee cup in hand, he raises it to me as he rounds the marble island to greet me. He dips his head, brushing his lips lightly over mine before smiling against them. “Good morning, beautiful. Coffee with cream and vanilla syrup for you, breakfast will be ready soon”. I smile back up at him like a dopey idiot, making him grin even wider back at me.

He hands the cup over to me and I bring it to my mouth, the sweet scent filling my nostrils and as I take a sip a small moan slips out, and I instantly regret it when I hear him chuckling in front of me. My eyes shoot up to his, and there's little lines creasing the sides of his eyes making him look that little bit older than he is. Not that I care, he could be fifty and I'd still want to fuck him, he looks *that* good in the mornings.

I roll my eyes at him hiding my smile with my cup, and turn to take a seat on one of the stools at the breakfast bar whilst he moves back over to the stove top to finish the bacon and eggs, and whilst he's cooking, I have a little nosey around from my seat, and wow his kitchen is beautiful. The kitchen cupboards are black with dark grey marble countertops around the edge of the room, a matching island in the middle with cushioned black stools that my ass fits comfortably into. Jaxx is finishing up cooking on the large gas stove as he speaks, “I hope this is okay for you. I wasn't prepared for company, but I remember you used to like this” he’s mostly concentrating on the food in the pan but peaks his head over his shoulder to check I’m listening.

I smile to myself remembering how he used to cook for Lily, Tristan and me when we were younger, and our parents were away leaving them in charge.

Tristan was absolutely useless in the kitchen, so Jaxx used to come stay with us to cook everything, and I think I enjoyed those meals the best. “I’m happy to eat whatever you cook, it's always good.”

He snorts out a laugh, “Yeah your brother was useless at cooking back when we were kids, and it definitely helped improve my skills”. When he turns and reaches up to grab some plates from the shelf, his muscles flex in his arms and torso turning my mouth dry. I'm staring at him like an imbecile, my mouth slightly open when he turns back to me and his lips turn up into a small smirk. “Enjoying the view over there?”

I lean onto my arms and over the counter a little to get a better peak at him, squinting my eyes a little. “Eh, you'll do” I say as I slide my ass back in my chair, unable to stop my lips tugging up into a smile. His mouth drops open in mock shock, a frown marring his beautiful face. I can't help but laugh at him as he looks like a lost puppy. But he doesn't stay like that for long as he quickly rounds the island to grab me, tickling my sides until I'm crying with laughter. “Take that back missy, I think you'll find I'll more than do”.

“Never!” I laugh harder at him but let out a little squeal as he picks me up and props me on the kitchen counter. I'm breathing heavily, my eyes darting between the steely greys that are swimming with mischief, but when he leans in close to my face I quickly sober. His body is between my legs which I have wrapped around his own, and his lips brush up against mine causing heat to pool at my core, as he whispers against my lips “Take it back or you'll be in big trouble”.

I feel my body reacting to him, but before I get a chance to get my bearings, I feel his hands sliding up my bare thighs, rounding my ass that's splayed on the countertop. I'm getting flashbacks from the previous night, his hands all over my body, me coming with his name on my lips. "Grace?" Jaxx prompts, bringing me back to the present, where I feel his fingertips pressing into my ass cheeks.

I look up to him feeling confident "And what if I don't want to take it back?" I lift a brow up at him sucking on my bottom lip, my teeth firmly digging into it. His hand comes up to my face, pulling my bottom lip from my mouth with a pop "Only I'm allowed to bite those pretty pink lips, you got that?" "I…"

My sentence is interrupted by someone knocking at the door, causing me to jump slightly. Jaxx drops his head and shakes it a little before straightening. "Looks like we'll have to revisit this conversation later baby girl". He quickly presses a kiss to my lips, wraps his arms around me and pulls me off the counter to stand, before walking to the door to see who's disturbed our cosy little morning.

I decide to make myself useful and plate out the breakfast whilst he's dealing with whoever is at the door. But that's soon interrupted when Jaxx's mom walks into the kitchen. She spots me instantly and if she's shocked, she doesn't show it as she rounds the island to give me a hug. "Grace honey, I wasn't expecting to find you here on a Sunday morning". her head flits back to Jaxx as if she's scolding him a little and he frowns back at her.

"That's because people usually call instead of turning up at people's houses unannounced mom". He's trying to stay calm, but I can tell she's got him a little riled up by her unexpected drop in. She pulls back from me and waves a hand at him dismissing his comment, "Oh Jaxx you never complain about my visits, why start now". He shoots her a look before shaking his head and walking over to where we're standing.

"Unfortunately mom, we're just about to grab a quick bite and then head out for the day. What did you call round for?" She looks back at him giving a slightly perplexed look, as if the idea of him binning her off to spend the day with me is ridiculous. "Oh, well I was calling round to spend some time with you, but I can see where I'm not wanted so I'll take my leave and speak to you in the week".

He lets out a groan and calls out to her as she's turning to leave. "Mom, you know you're overreacting, I'll call you later and we'll have lunch this week. Just next time please call ahead to check I'm not busy". She nods and turns her head towards me, "No worries, my bad. I can certainly see I've disturbed your morning, speak to you soon, lovely to see you again Grace". With that she's out the kitchen and nearing the front door before Jaxx sighs and goes after her to say goodbye.

By the time he's back in the kitchen, I've plated up the bacon and eggs and have sat at the island where it's set for us to eat breakfast. He comes to join me sitting beside me before picking up his knife and fork, letting out a breath he turns to me slightly. "I'm sorry about that, she can be a bit much sometimes and I don't want her to overwhelm you".

I snort a laugh. "Yeah, I doubt I'm in her good graces when the first time she sees me in years, I'm standing half naked in her son's kitchen". He barks out a laugh, realising the situation we were in, and shakes his head a little as if clearing his thoughts.

"Well, how about after breakfast we head back to your house, you can get sorted and if you're feeling up to it, I still have that little date planned out for us. But if you'd rather me just drop you back home and see me another day, then I can do that too". I smile over to him, finding I'm suddenly excited for the day.

"That date sounds good to me".

....

It's almost 11am by the time we make it out of the house and to mine, someone from Jaxx's work came to drop his car for him so that we didn't need to worry about sorting it, but now all I have to worry about is what to say to Hallie and Rose.

We pull up to the front of my house and Jaxx turns in his seat to face me. "I'll leave you here for a little while, I'll need to fill out a few bits of paperwork from last night, and you'll eventually need to do a statement, but I can get that from you at some point". He leans into me brushing his lips against mine in a light kiss. "I'll come back at one, so you should have enough time to speak to the girls and get sorted but if you want longer, then just text me, okay?" I nod in agreement before turning to get out of the car, when he speaks again "Oh, before you go. I didn't have a chance to ask last night, but did you know that guy that attacked you?"

I freeze momentarily looking back over my shoulder to him before nodding, his body stiffens slightly and his jaw tenses. "Yeah, kind of, Hallie goes running with him and two other friends, they invited us to join their table last night. I don't think she would've ever thought that one of them could be like that". I really need to speak to Hallie though and clear things up.

"Okay, it's fine, I just wanted to check. You get in and sorted and I'll see you in a little while". With one last kiss I jump out of the car and head to the front door, hoping they're both already up so I can find out what went on after I left, and most importantly if Hallie had any idea about the type of guy Josh was.

I call out to them both as I enter the house and make my way to the kitchen to pour some water and hear them both barrelling down the stairs to get to me. "Grace. Oh my god. Thank god you're ok. Jaxx text me off your phone and we've been worried sick all night about you. Come sit down and tell us what happened. Who the fuck hurt you?"

I follow them both to the living room taking a seat on the sofa, both of them either side of me, and sit back into it. "It was Josh, he um, must have followed me out of the bar.. And he.. He cornered me and dragged me down an alleyway and tried to attack me". I let out a shaky breath before continuing. "I think Jaxx was on patrol, and thankfully he saw what happened and got to me just in time". I feel a tear slipping from my eye and quickly wipe it away not wanting to cry anymore. I'm so done with being the victim.

Hallie puts her arm around me "Oh honey, I don't even know what to say. I'm so sorry that we went and sat with them now. I wondered where he had gone to, but the other guys said he does that all the time and assumed he'd gone home, so I didn't put two and two together. I'll stop going running with them, I don't want to give them the wrong idea". I look back to my friend, she looks sad for me, but I don't want her to be. "Hallie, it's not your fault he wasn't raised right, and I don't want you to stop running with them on my account, you seemed to be getting on really well with one of them. I just wish I had been more careful. I was texting Jaxx and not paying attention to who was around me or what was going on". She runs her hand up and down my arm a couple more times, before pulling back and scowling a little, "Don't even think for one minute that I'll continue seeing a guy with friends like that. I'll set the record straight with him because you come first".

Rose huffs then, and I sneak a glance out of the corner of my eye at her, "Don't either of you feel bad for that fucking jerk, I hope he gets what's coming to him. I'm just glad you're ok Grace". I smile back at her, "Thanks Rose, I'm just glad it wasn't any worse. Jaxx is going to the station now to do paperwork and then coming back here for me. He planned a date for today and I'll be damned if I let this ruin anything".

We carry on talking for a little while about what's going on for us the rest of the week, and then I go to get ready for another date with Jaxx.

15

Jaxx

It sucked leaving Grace at her house this morning, but I needed to get to the station and deal with this absolute shit show. Josh, I'd finally learned his name this morning, was being held in one of the cells, and now demanding a lawyer. He could fucking have one, but Mike had already checked for me and found cameras on the building seeing him dragging Grace away, and then there was the fact us two officers had witnessed what happened, he wasn't getting away with jack shit, and I'd find as many charges as I could to add to it. I've barely been sitting at my desk for five minutes, going over the paperwork, when Mike pokes his head in the door. "How's Grace after last night?" I look up at him, noticing the furrow in his brow and the genuine concern etched across his face.

I let out a long sigh and prop my hand under my chin, supporting it as I glance back down at the statement in front of me that I'm struggling to fill out. "She's surprisingly okay. I just dropped her back at her place for a couple of hours while I try to sort this out. Has he spoken at all?"

Mike shifts his weight, still standing in the doorway, his eyes soft with concern. I know I'm going to have to pass the case off to Mike with it being a conflict of interest, but I need to know *something.* "Nah, he's refusing to say anything. But his lawyer is on the way, so once he's here I'll get him interviewed, and charged". Good, the quicker that happens the better. I don't want her thinking about it any longer than necessary, I nod in thanks to him, and he darts back out the room to deal with his day.

I try like hell for the next two hours to concentrate on anything, but my head is on a constant roll, filled with thoughts of Grace. How scared she was when I got to her, to how we ended up in my bed. I let out a groan, and my head falls back against the desk chair, my thoughts taking a wrong turn causing my dick to go hard as a rock, because I still taste her sweetness in my mouth. Remembering what she felt like, and wanting to do it again, *now.* By 12.45pm I'm out the door and heading back over to Grace's house for the date I promised her, I changed it slightly but I couldn't be away from her the rest of the day, so things got changed up. There is an autumn fair that's just come into town, and I know she could do with something fun to take her mind off things, and so that's where we are headed for the afternoon.

I'm not waiting long outside her front door, when it swings open and she's stood in front of me looking as beautiful as ever. Her hair is tied back in a messy ponytail, small tendrils have fallen out of it and frame her heart shaped face. She's got minimal makeup on and is wearing a pair of dungarees paired with a simple t-shirt underneath, a knit cardigan thrown over the top and a pair of classic Vans on her feet. She looks good. Too good.

I eye her up and down appreciatively, and when my eyes make their way back to her face, she's got a gorgeous little flush of pink covering her usually creamy cheeks. Leaning into her I wrap an arm around her waist and pull her close to me as my face comes down to meet hers. “You look good enough to eat sweetheart. But we have an afternoon to enjoy so I'll save that for another time”, I say shooting her a wink as my lips find hers.

When I pull back, she’s grinning at me, with a smile that bright it makes my heart melt. *God I love this girl.* I'm not even scared about telling her that, because the truth is I'm so in love with her it's not even funny. It feels like a small obsession that’s developed over the years and grown into this ache I feel when I'm not with her. I missed her so much when she was gone, and part of me is slightly terrified she's going to leave me again.

Right now though I need to focus on the present, and so I tamper down my thoughts and take her hand in mine and head to the car. The fair doesn't take too long to get to, but it’s busy and we spend a little while trying to park, but once we do, we’re at the booth buying tickets to get in.

She's smiling, looking around and I use that moment to drink her in. I wasn't sure if she'd like this idea, but it was a simple way for us to spend time together, and right now I can't seem to get enough of this girl. “This is such a lovely idea, us coming here. I love the fairs and I’ve missed them with being away, it’s a nice little way to remind me why I love it here”. *Thank fucking god.* My smile gets bigger at that as I wrap my arm around her shoulder pressing a kiss to the top of her head.

"Well get used to this baby girl. Because I'll do anything short of jumping out of a plane to spend time with you". She pouts at me and frowns a little, big eyes looking up at me "Oh damn, that's what I wanted to do for our next date". I actually think she's being serious for a minute with the look on her face, but then she turns to me and I spot her lip tugging up into a cheeky grin as she bumps me with her hip. "I'm just joking ha. Can you imagine". She does a dramatic shiver, and I can't help the laugh that bursts out of me as I tighten my grip around her.

I bring my lips close to her ear so she can hear me "I always thought you were a little daredevil but maybe I was wrong". She's giggling back at me when we hear the shrill voice of Alice Smith behind us, "Oh isn't this cosy, didn't take you as the type to date your friends' siblings Jaxx". My gaze slides to her, wishing it could be anyone else, and I'm about to respond when Grace takes the lead "Didn't take you for such a nosey bitch *Alice,* but oh look here we are. Why don't you get lost and find some other gossip to sink your teeth into".

I try my hardest to hold my laughter in, but Alice's face is a picture. Her blonde bob is swishing across her face as her eyes dart between Grace and me, the shock on her face apparent as she tries to come to terms with someone standing up to her, and for once she's actually lost for words, but Grace isn't quite done yet, "Go on run along now, your minions are waiting". She must decide the better option is to abort the mission, because she huffs out a breath, turns on her heel and stomps away. I manage to hold it together for a moment, but the instant my eyes land on Grace, laughter bubbles up from deep inside me. My shoulders shake with it as she peeks up at me, grinning like a Cheshire cat.

I lean back into her, wrapping my arms around her waist again, nuzzling my head into the warmth of her neck. "Well, I didn't take you for such a feisty one, Grace. Almost saw the claws there". She peeks up at me, her eyes twinkling from the laughter. "Felt good to finally tell her, once and for all". I smile down at her, squeezing her a little tighter. "C'mon, let's go have some fun".

We spend the next while hitting every ride she can possibly handle, laughing and screaming our way through the park. By the time we make our way over to the food stands, the sun is starting to dip, painting the sky in streaks of orange and pink. We're scanning the stands when I feel her stiffen beside me. I glance down, searching for what's wrong, but she's frozen—her body tense, her green eyes wide, staring straight ahead as if she's seen a ghost.

I look around quickly but can't see what she must be looking at, so I nudge her a little to get her attention "Grace, sweetheart what's wrong?" Her head snaps up to me and she blinks a couple of times before shaking her head. "Nothing, I just… Nothing, it's fine. What do you want to eat?" But now I feel like I'm on alert, because she's clearly seen something that's scared her. "It's not nothing Grace, what's got you freezing up like that. What did you see?"

I turn her body towards me but she’s avoiding my gaze, and I can't just let it slide now so I put my hand under her chin and tip her head up towards me. “Tell me Grace, what's going on?” She lets out a sigh, her eyes closing slightly. “I thought I saw Liam, but as quick as I saw him, he was gone. It's probably just my mind playing tricks on me after this whole nightmare this week”. My head shoots up to look around for him, his picture now etched into my memory, but there’s so many people here that he’d be long gone now.

I wouldn’t put it past him to turn up in town, but I’d have expected him to show up at her door, so it feels off that she’d spot him here, of all places, at the fair. Either way, I want us out of here as quickly as possible. I glance down at Grace again, trying to keep my voice steady, though the alarm in my chest is harder to hide. I smooth my features, forcing a calm expression before I speak. "Okay, don’t worry. I’ll keep an eye out for him. Let’s just grab something to eat and head back to the car. We can eat there. How does that sound?” She relaxes slightly, nodding at me, but I can feel the tension still coiling in her. I let her pick what she wants—my appetite long gone—and we make our way to a stand. We grab our food quickly, then head toward the car, the whole time, I’m watching every shadow, every person that passes by.

16

Grace

The weekend feels like all but a distant memory by the time Monday morning rolls around. I'm anxious but excited to be finally starting my new job and I woke up way too early. The sun is just rising over the lake, and I enjoy the view as I sip on my coffee at the kitchen island feeling extra ready for the day in my new pant-suit. I haven't got to be at the office for another hour or so and I'm well ahead of schedule, thinking I might even walk to work since it's such a nice morning.

When I woke up and drew the curtains this morning, the sunshine put me in a good mood for the day and I spent the morning enjoying my good mood. By the time I'm finishing my coffee Rose is rushing down the stairs, late as per usual. I don't think I've ever met anyone to be as disorganised as her.

She looks like she could do with a coffee, so I pour one in her to go mug so that she has something to wake her up for the morning. Holding it out to her, she gives me a tired smile and comes to give me a tight squeeze before taking the mug from my hands. "You don't understand how grateful I am for this right now. I overslept and I have to fly to Seattle for a big meeting this morning for a new job I'm hoping to take on".

She's an awesome baker and I know she's going to absolutely smash it, I give her some of my good mood for morning encouragement, "You're going to be fine. Just take a minute to breathe and get your bearings before you head out, and if you don't get it, well then, it's their loss". I give her my brightest smile and push as much confidence as I can her way.

She taps her finger on my nose and playfully scrunches her eyes a little at me, "I'm stealing some of your chirpiness today. I'm gonna need it, wish me luck". She's out the door before I even manage to utter a goodbye to her, I linger around in the kitchen and clean up a little before heading out the door.

The walk this morning was a good call. It's crisp and fresh, and the sun is just adding to my good mood, but as I round the corner about half a mile from home, I feel like something is off as I crane my neck slightly hearing a car, and notice someone has begun following me slowly. It's hanging back a little, and I'd normally not notice things like that but after last week I'm feeling more alert than usual. I try to brush it off as a coincidence but the way it's slowly trailing behind me has me on edge, sliding my phone out of my pocket as I'm turning to cross the road, I snap a quick picture of it.

Whoever the driver is must see because they put their foot down and speed off down the nearest street, confirming my suspicion that I was definitely being followed so I pick up the pace and almost run to work, checking behind me every minute.

By the time I reach the office I'm a hot mess, I dip into the bathroom to sort myself out before I start, and a quick look over myself has me cringing. My hair is sticking to my forehead slightly, and my face has started to look a little shiny from the clammy beads of sweat I see forming along my hairline. I dig around my bag looking for the small compact I usually carry, quickly fixing up my hair and face the best I can. I'm just so wound up still that my breathing feels like it's not quite settled back to normal, bracing my hands on the basin I take a closer look at myself in the mirror and give myself a little pep talk "Sort yourself out Grace. Today is a good day, you're fine, you're safe, nothing's going to hurt you".

I chant that last part a couple more times before taking a big gulp of air, straighten my jacket and find my way to the kitchen where Janet is preparing a cup of coffee, she peeks her head up from where she's stirring the mug and smile takes over her face when she spots me. "Good morning Grace, are you looking forward to your first day?" I smile back at her "Of course, I can't wait to get stuck in". "Great, I've left some bits on your desk to help you and there's a few of the team in already to help you if you get stuck, I'll show you to your desk when you're ready".

I quickly make my coffee up and follow her out to my desk where she sets me up with my new work and password. "Jack from accounting will head over shortly to help you get started". With that she turns and heads back to her desk and busies herself with the mound of paperwork that's waiting for her.

Once I've set myself up, I'm only waiting a little while before an older man in his forties approaches and introduces himself as Jack, he shows me through what

I need to do, and I get to work quickly getting to grips with the new systems. Hours pass by and before I know it, it's lunchtime, I grab my purse and head over to the deli across the street to grab some lunch. Having just ordered, my eyes wander out of the window to watch people getting about their day, when I spot the car that was following me this morning parked up just across the street. Panic takes over me as I search for my phone, pulling it out of my purse and call Jaxx, as I don't know what I should do in this situation, but his call goes to voicemail. *Shit*. He must be working.

Who the fuck would be following me? No it must be a coincidence, I tell myself as I turn back to the counter, trying to ignore the car sitting outside, I feel like I'm waiting forever for my order to come, but when it does, I chance a look over the street again but the car is gone. I shrug it off as best as I can but my fear spikes up again when I get back into the office and Janet turns to me smiling and points to the roses sitting on my desk. "You just had a delivery; a lovely bunch of flowers and it looks like there's a little card on them". I nod thanks to her and with shaky legs I head to my desk, plucking the card out of the flowers and opening it.

Enjoy your job, because you won't be there for long.
Missing you.
X

Fuck Fuck Fuck. I sit down in my chair, staring back at the flowers that I know can only come from one person. I'm in a daze for the rest of the afternoon, feeling like my first day is an absolute waste, and I get absolutely nothing done apart from panic about why Liam is taking these extreme lengths to get back with me.

When 5pm finally hits, I'm up and out of the office so quickly that I barely wave a goodbye to Janet, but I'm just not in the right headspace today and I don't quite know what to do, leaving the building I try to keep my wits about me as I make the 20-minute journey home. *Urgh why didn't I drive this morning!!* It's starting to go dark by the time I've left so it's even harder to stay alert. I'm listening to every sound, and in such deep concentration, that when my phone rings in my pocket it makes me jump.

Pulling it out I see Jaxx's name and answer it instantly, his voice filters through the phone, and I instantly feel a little of the anxiety leave "Hey sweetheart, Sorry I missed your call, I left my phone on my desk and I've been out of the station all day. What did you call for?"

I don't wait to tell him as I rush my words out, "I.. um. I think I'm being followed, I could be imagining things, but I've seen the same car twice today and I had another flower delivery just after lunch". Jaxx is silent on the phone for so long that I have pull my phone away from my face to check the call is still connected. "Jaxx? Are you still there?" "Fuck, yeah baby girl, I'm still here. I'm guessing you're thinking this is Liam too. *Shit*. I'm so sorry I never leave my phone, I could have come to the office and checked out the area".

I panic at the thought of everyone at the office knowing my business on my first day. “No, it’s fine. I don’t want everyone at work knowing what’s going on… I just started, and that’s the last thing I need on day one”. I take a deep breath, trying to steady myself. “Sorry, I know you want to help, but I’m just panicking a bit, and walking home isn’t helping”. “Shit, Grace, where are you? I’m coming to get you. You shouldn't walk anywhere by yourself right now”.

I hear the panic in his voice, and I try to calm him as quickly as I can. “It’s fine, I’m almost home. Just stay on the phone until I get there, and I’ll be fine. I’m literally two minutes away”.

There’s a long pause, then he sighs heavily into the phone. “I had my colleague look into him some more the other day. I’ll give him a call, and we’ll figure this out. But just promise me you’ll stay safe and be with someone at all times until we can get this issue sorted. I can have a patrol car near your house to keep an eye out until we find him”. “Jaxx I...” I start to protest, but he cuts me off before I can get the words out. “Don’t even try to tell me it’s not needed, Grace. You’re the most important person to me, and other than cuffing you to me all day, I need to ensure your safety. There will be a patrol car parked outside keeping watch tonight. End of discussion!” Oh, shit. He’s pissed now, I can hear the anger in his voice. But I’m furious, too—he’s treating me like I need a fucking babysitter.

I huff into the phone, my tone sharp. “Fine, whatever. But I don’t need a fucking babysitter, Jaxx. I’m home now, so I’ll speak to you later”. I pull the phone away from my face and end the call, slamming my finger on the end button angrily and cutting him off mid-sentence. My blood is boiling. I can't believe he thinks I need someone watching over me 24/7 like some damsel in distress.

I stomp up the stairs to my room, still fuming, and pull on my pyjamas. The weight of the day starts to hit me, and I need something to calm my nerves. Without a second thought, I head back downstairs in search of a bottle of wine from the fridge. I'm not usually a weekday drinker, but tonight… fuck it, I need it.

I settle on the sofa with my book, trying to distract myself. I'm barely ten minutes into reading when the doorbell rings, and my head shoots towards the door wondering who the hell is calling this late? I get up, irritation bubbling in my chest, and open the door. Standing there, arms crossed, and jaw clenched, is a rather pissed off looking Jaxx who looks like he's about to explode.

"Don't fucking hang up on me ever again, baby girl."

Oh, fuck.

17

Grace

We stand in some sort of face off, seeing who breaks first, but obviously it ends up being me. I scoff turning to walk back into my house, Jaxx hot on my heels "I don't know why you bothered coming here. I'm not in the mood for you tonight, you seriously pissed me off implying that I need a babysitter Jaxx. I'm not a kid, I'm a grown woman who can look after herself".

"What, like you managed to last weekend?" His words hit me like a punch to the gut and I stop short, my body frozen in place. I spin on my heel to face him, my anger spiking, hotter than before. He realizes his mistake almost immediately and backtracks, softening his tone a little. "Shit, Grace I didn't mean it like that, I just.." He trails off running his hands down his face, huffing out a sigh "I just want you safe and all you're doing is pushing back against me, can you just be a little flexible with me here?"

I square my shoulders, giving him a dirty look as I try to tamp down some of the anger, but it's no use "Why Jaxx, I'm not some fragile little doll that you need to protect, I managed perfectly fine by myself all this time without *you,* and now you come marching in here making demands and expecting me to follow", it comes out a little shrill and probably a bit mean as I jab a finger at his chest, the frustration and anger pouring out of me, but he doesn't budge. Instead, he crowds me, stepping closer, slowly backing me against the wall in the hallway. I feel the heat of his body closing in, his presence suffocating.

His arms come up to cage me in, framing either side of my head, and I'm so close to him I can almost taste his breath. "Do you not think I know that? God damn it Grace, do you not think I hated not knowing if you were safe or not?" His voice drops lower, raw and heavy with emotion. "You consume my thoughts more than I should probably admit by now. I feel like I want to lock you up in the house to keep you safe, but I know I can't do that. So please, for God's sake, just fucking listen and let me help".

My hearts pounding in my chest as I just stare back at him lost for words, my breathing becomes choppy as I feel the heat unfurling inside me, *why the fuck is this turning me on so much.* I try to push back against him but it's no use, he's got me boxed in and I feel slightly trapped, but I refuse to let him see me as any weaker than I already am.

I steel myself pushing my chin up and stare him dead in the eyes "I don't fucking want babysitters Jaxx, stop pushing this. I don't need someone watching me like I'm some pathetic little girl". His eyes narrow in on me "Then move in with me so that I can keep you safe, he won't know where you are then at least".

My anger morphs into pure shock as I stare back at him, but I quickly smooth my features as my eyes narrow in on him, pushing back at his chest a little harder "The fuck am I moving in with you when you're acting like a caveman. I think it’s best if you leave. And don't send a patrol car round”.

He doesn't want to listen to me though and gets impossibly closer, his lips brushing my cheek. “I'm going nowhere baby girl, and if you would stop being so fucking stubborn and just let me help, we wouldn't be arguing about this right now”. He pauses for a second, clearly not done with what he's saying, “I know I'm coming off as overprotective right now, maybe even a little possessive, and I’m really not trying to be. I’ve spent over half my life looking out for you, and I'm not about to stop now just because you're a grown woman. I need to do this not only for your safety, but for my sanity”.

I want to push him away so badly, my body is craving him more than my brain right now though, so I try the next best thing and voice how desperately I need him to drop this, but my voice betrays me too “Please Jaxx” I whimper “Please just let it go”.

His hand comes down to cup my face and I involuntarily lean into him, “You know I can't do that Grace; I need you safe so can you please just compromise a little”. His eyes flit around the house slightly, as if assessing the space, but he makes no move to separate from me, “Where are the girls?”

I gulp, my throat tight with unease. *Fuck* there’s no getting around this, “They're um.. they're both away, and won’t be back for a few days”. He looks back down to me, his features relaxing a little more as he lets out a defeated sigh and rests his head against mine. After a few seconds, he moves against me and takes a deep breath, preparing himself for the next part of out little battle "Fine you have two choices if you don't want the car, you stay with me or I stay here with you, pick one".

I feel my anger resurface as he lists out his demands again, and I push back against him once more, "No Jaxx just stop I don't need watching! I'm not some fucking flight risk". His hand comes around my face and under my jaw gripping it just a tiny bit and lifting it to face him. "Pick one, or I'll pick it for you". "No!" I shout back, and he leans in close again, his lips almost brushing mine, "Fine I'm staying here with you".

I want to push him away again, but his intoxicating scent draws me in, and I have to admit this protective side is turning me on, I'm still trying not to crack though, deciding I should push my luck one last time, "Why are you doing this, why are you so bothered?" He pulls back slightly bringing both hands up now to cup my face in his huge palms, his thumb stroking my cheek, and his beautiful grey eyes searching between mine. His tongue darts out to swipe across his bottom lip and I get the urge to bite it, *Not now Grace, you're in the middle of a fight.*

He looks like he's weighing something in his mind, deciding whether to tell me the truth or keep it to himself. After a long pause, he finally speaks, his voice barely above a whisper as he utters the words I have craved to hear for so long.

"Because I'm in love with you."

18

Jaxx

Fuck, I shouldn't have just said that. The look on her face is a mixture of shock and fear, and I'm not helping the situation one bit, acting like an absolute dick because she just won't listen to me, but I can't take it back now, and she'll just have to deal with it. Her perfect lips part ever so slightly, those bright green eyes flitting between the two of mine, searching for some sort of answer I'm not even sure I have. "W.. What?" It comes out as almost a whisper, but she's clearly still trying to process what I just said so I say it again, "I'm in love with you Grace. I have been for a very long time, and the sooner you know that the better".

She swallows as she struggles to process the words I'm feeding her, then as if she's come back down to earth again her face turns back angry, her eyes narrowing in on me once more as her eyebrows pinch together, "No! You don't get to do that. You don't get to be a dick and then say you love me. That's not fair. Leave". She's shoving back at me again and if I were a smarter man, I'd turn and walk out the door and just arrange for a patrol car to sit outside her house.

But I'm not, so I get in her face again grabbing at her arms, maybe a little too hard because she winces slightly, but I'm so wound up right now that she's being such a little brat, I want to shake her a little to make her see just how stupid she's being, leaving herself so vulnerable, my voice rises a little coming out sharp and firm as I try to talk some sense into her, "Grace! For fucks sake, I'm not fucking telling you that to be a dick. You want the truth and you have it. I fucking love you, have done for years, and I'm not prepared to take any chances when it comes to your safety". We lock eyes and all brain function leaves my head as I drink her in, eyes wide, lips slightly parted, looking a little flushed as her heavy breathing matches mine, and all I can think is *fuck it..*

My lips crash down on hers, hard. I need her safe and she's winding me up, so if she won't listen to me, I'll show her how much she means to me. She doesn't respond for a moment and I think I've fucked everything up by being just a little too forceful with her, but as I'm about to pull back she responds to me like she's got on the same page as me *finally.* She lets out a little moan, and I take full advantage of it by pushing my tongue into her mouth, a silent battle between us over who has the most power right now.

My hand comes up to cup the back of her neck, the other snakes around her waist pulling her closer to me, or me closer to her I'm not really sure right now. All I know is I need her, desperately. Pressing her up against the wall, I wedge my leg between hers to push her legs apart a little and press her body into the wall.

My dick grows impossibly hard being this close and feeling her, hearing those breathy little moans as she takes what I'm giving her. Manicured fingers grab at my shirt likes she's desperate for me, but she clearly isn't too sure if she wants this right now, because she pulls back abruptly, Pink swollen lips parted and face flushed, she's breathing heavily, her eyes darting between mine, "Jaxx", she pants out "I don't want to argue with you but…"

I silence her by pressing a kiss to her lips, we don't need to talk about it anymore tonight, because I'm not fucking leaving her whether she likes it or not. "I know Grace, I'm not trying to argue with you, I just need you to try and compromise a little and understand where I'm coming from. But right now, I just need to feel you, please". Her eyes search mine once more before she gives up her internal battle and our lips crash once more.

I slide my hands down her body, stopping just below her ass and haul her up into my arms, as she lets out a little squeal in shock, her flimsy pyjamas not doing much to cover her perfect nipples poking out through them while her legs instinctively wrap around me. I turn us, marching up the stairs to get to her room, "Which room is yours?" I breathe out in between kisses, and she points to the room on the left.

Pushing the door open, I walk us quickly to the bed and drop her down onto it. She bounces a little before falling back onto her elbows, I lean down crowding her again, my hands either side of her curvy little body. "Tell me if you want me to stop, baby, because I need you so badly right now that unless you tell me, I won't be able to control myself".

She shakes her head at me like I’m a fucking mind reader and know what she’s trying to say, so I pinch at her hips a little, leaning in even closer “Words baby, use them”. Her eyes flit up to mine quickly before coming back down to look at my shirt, her tongue darting out and licking her lips, I let out a groan and my head falls against hers. “Don't stop, I want you. I need you too”. It's barely a whisper and I almost don't hear it from the blood pounding in my ears, but my brain catches up as a slow smile creeps across my face.

“Good, then be a good girl and do as I say”. I don't give her time to react as I drag her hips down the bed closer to me, pressing my hips into the pathetic excuse of shorts she's wearing so that she can feel just how much I want her. “Do you feel that baby, feel what you do to me, you drive me fucking crazy with that smart mouth of yours”.

Her breathing gets heavier, lips slightly parted as she stares back at me, her mind working as she tries to decide if she should talk back to me right now. My fingers dip into the waistband of her shorts as I begin to slide them down her legs, realising then she's not wearing any panties. *Good.* I come down to my knees at the bottom of the bed, leaning into her warmth and enjoying the view of those perfect pink lips, wet and ready for me.

Shyness seems to overtake her, softening her expression as a light blush covers her cheeks, the earlier anger fading to something hesitant and vulnerable as she tries to pull her knees together, cutting off my new favourite view, I press my hands onto her knees to push them back apart. “Keep your legs still or I’ll use my cuffs to keep them apart". Her blush deepens, she's clearly not used to me being so forward and demanding with her, but this is the version she gets of me now, she'll get used to it eventually, because I am a man obsessed.

She doesn't move, keeping her legs wide open for me, watching me, waiting for me to do something else to her, "Is this all for me?" I ask, running two fingers through her slit as I gather her wetness up onto them, before putting them in my mouth to taste her. *Fuck she tastes so good.* When she doesn't respond instantly I raise my brow at her, silently urging her to respond, she nods quickly before remembering her voice, "Yes." She breathes it out and I smirk at her,

"Good because, I've been desperate for another taste of you since Saturday night".

19

Grace

I've never got to experience this version of Jaxx, but Jesus, I can certainly get used to it. My brain function must be working at about 5% right now, because I can't focus on anything other than the feel of his hands on me. I can't breathe, my whole body is on fire and he's being too fucking slow, I need more from him, and he must notice because when I let out a frustrated sigh, his hands come back up to grip my inner thighs.

His mouth moves to press feather light kisses against me as he works his way towards my centre, when he gets there his tongue darts out and licks up my slit in one long stroke, I cry out and my hips to buck up into him, he's holding me firmly in place so I'm unable to get the friction I desperately need, I just writhe under him instead, trying to get whatever I can from him somehow but it's no use, his hold is strong keeping me in place.

I know he's doing it on purpose because he peeks back up to me and lets out a little laugh making me narrow my eyes at him once more this evening, "It's not fucking funny Jaxx, you're being too slow, I need you to go faster". He clicks his tongue at me shaking his head, “Patience baby girl, I'm taking my time with you right now, because when I'm inside of you I intend to ruin you for any other man”. I want to be offended by what he's saying but he just turns me on more, I let out a breathy moan and he takes that as cue to continue.

He starts slowly working his tongue up and down me, drawing torturous circles over my clit. I’m crying out wanting him to stop and continue all at the same time, when he slips a finger inside me and pushes it against my walls in a come-hither motion, doing this a few times before adding a second finger, working in and out of me until I feel myself building up to my release. He must feel my muscles clenching slightly as he works his fingers into me harder, pushing his mouth against my clit a little firmer, nipping and biting at the sensitive flesh there.

“AHH, Jaxx!! Fuckkk” I can barely get my words out as my orgasm takes over my body, my legs begin to shake as I struggle to stay still beneath him. I feel the blood rush to my head, unable to hear a thing over the pounding of it running through my ears, but the clinking of his his belt buckle hitting the floor has my head shooting up, my eyes meeting his, I draw my attention to his fingers that work unbuttoning his shirt as he slides it off his toned shoulders and throws it onto the chair behind him, kicking his shoes off and dropping his trousers to the floor. His boxers are the next thing to go, and my eyes bug out of my head at the sight in front of me.

“Jesus fucking Christ Jaxx! That thing will not fit in me”. I try to shuffle back up the bed a little because his dick is fucking huge, and I am not taking the chance that thing will fit. I thought it was big when I felt him the other day, but this is next level. Before I get far enough away from him, his hands dart out and grab my ankles holding me in place, he’s clearly enjoying himself because his dick does a little twitch like he's making it dance for me. I bring my eyes up to meet his face which winds me up more because he has the biggest fucking grin ever.

“What, this little guy?” He asks, wrapping his hand around it and pumping a few times with his fist. He's on the bed faster than I can blink, pulling my top over my head, then pushing down on me with his naked body and I happily oblige. His lips come crashing back down on mine, whilst one hand comes up to play with my nipple, working me up a little more. I all but forget about his massive dick until I feel him pushing against my entrance and I prepare myself to take him in, but he stops suddenly, pulling back and sitting on his heels. “Fuck” he whispers to himself, but not quiet enough that I don't hear him too, because I'm instantly on alert and sitting, coming to his level.

“What? What is it?” He looks down at himself then back up to me, “Condom. I don't have one, and I can bet you don't either since you came back here to escape men”. I think for a second, having a mental debate as to whether what I’m about to come out with is a good idea or if it will send him running for the hills. “I.. I'm on birth control, but I can go find some” the smile that takes over his face helps to clear some of the tension I was feeling a moment ago when he leans back into me, his grin getting impossibly bigger, “Fuck no baby, I don't want anything between us right now, so

I'm good if you are". I nod to him quickly, trying to hide my impatience as his arm comes under my leg to give himself more access to me, but before I can figure out what he's going to do next, he rams into me, stilling as soon as he's inside. "You okay sweetheart?"

I'm pretty sure he's just sucked all the wind out of me as my wide eyes catch his slightly panicked ones, and it takes me a minute to catch my breath, I quickly nod back to him, but he growls back a little "Words Grace, are you okay?" "Yes" I breathe out "Start moving please" I push my hips up into him a little, causing him to let out a breathy laugh, he pulls back out a little and then rams himself back into me again.

I feel so full from him, but it's worth every inch I take as he pounds into me and picks up the pace a little once he's fully gotten his rhythm, I feel the pressure building again and find myself getting right to the edge, but just as soon as I feel it he pulls out of me and flips me, pushing my legs up so that I'm on all fours.

His body presses into mine as he leans over me bringing his lips to my ear, "I'm going to enjoy every minute of this tonight. I've waited so fucking long for you". I twist my head over my shoulder slightly to get a good look at him, smirking back as I raise a brow "Well hurry up and fuck me already" I say as I wiggle my ass at him a little. Shaking his head, he lets out a little huff and murmurs "Brat", quickly lining himself back up with me he rams into me so hard I almost scream, but he grabs my head and pushes me down into the pillow, so that my cries become muffled whilst he's pounding into me.

His hands come down and grip my hips that hard I'm sure he's going to leave bruises, but I don't care right now, he could be this rough all of the time, and I'd probably enjoy it. A hand comes around to the front of my body and between my legs as he uses the pads of his fingers to massage my clit again, slowing his movements but taking himself impossibly further inside of me. “Fuck baby, we’re so good together, are you gonna come for me again?” The feeling of him, and the words he's giving me has me crying out loudly as my orgasm takes over my body. He follows shortly after, spilling his seed inside me as he falls against me, his arms keeping him from falling on me until he slowly pulls out and rolls onto his side. I collapse next to him, my breathing struggling to return to normal.

He looks over to my dishevelled form and reaches over to tuck a stray hair behind my ear smoothing the rest down as he goes, he leans up onto his arm and presses a kiss to my head, “Back in a second”, he says as he gets up from the bed and goes to the bathroom, coming back a minute later with a warm cloth and I go to take it from him. He pulls his hand back shaking his head at me, “Let me take care of you”. I nod slowly, not having had someone do this before, but I enjoy care and attention he puts into the simple task.

My eyes begin to drift shut as he moves himself off the bed, and I quickly climb into bed, but when I feel the bed dip, I open them again to see him climbing in with me. I expected him to be getting dressed, preparing to leave, but instead, he’s gently tugging at the covers, tucking us both in. Confusion washes over me as I try to understand what he's doing, and he must see it in my eyes. For a moment, he mirrors my expression, then he's reaching for me and pulls me close, his warmth wrapping around me like his needs this too "I told you I'm not leaving you alone, and you wouldn't come to mine, so I'm staying with you until you either let me get a car outside or you come to mine".

He presses a kiss to my head as his sturdy arm wraps around me, I begin to protest but he holds up his hand "Stop trying to fight me on this, it's happening whether you like it or not, so close your eyes and go to sleep baby girl, we'll talk in the morning, I love you". I don't respond because as much as I know I do in fact love him, I don't know if I'm ready to open my heart up to someone again so soon, even if I have loved him my entire adult life. I know he doesn't expect the words back so soon, so I snuggle in closer to him and drift off to sleep.

20

Grace

I must have forgotten to close my curtains last night, because the morning sun beams through the window pulling me from the most beautiful sleep, the dull beeping from my alarm in the distance. I move to shuffle and sit up, but I'm stopped by a huge arm that's draped over my waist. Looking over my shoulder to the owner of the arm, I drink in his sleeping form.

Brow furrowed slightly as if he's deep in thought and lips pulled into a tight line. I try to move his arm to get myself out of bed and ready for work, but his grip tightens on me dragging me closer to him. He breathes in deeply, inhaling my scent and snuggles in further to me, pulling me into his cocoon of warmth. "Stop trying to escape me baby, cause I'm not letting you go". I smile to myself, enjoying this side to him, "Well you're gonna have to because I'm going to be late for work, and it's my second day so if I'm late then it's your fault".

He groans into me, holding on tighter for a moment but finally relents and lets go, rolling onto his back and propping his arm behind his head which causes his biceps bulge a little. I avert my gaze quickly otherwise I'll get distracted and jump back into bed, and rush into the bathroom to start the shower, letting it warm whilst I brush my teeth. Once it's at temperature, I jump in and start washing my hair, I'm in my own little world as the door opens after a minute and Jaxx steps into the mist with me. "What are you doing?" I screech, he turns to look at me and deadpans "Getting a shower, what does it look like?"

I let out a groan, "Can you not wait until I'm done?" He slowly looks me up and down as a smirk tips up on one side of his face, I look down to be greeted by his dick standing to attention, my eyes snap back up to meet his as I start shaking my head, whining "I'm going to be late, get out". That just seems to egg him on further as he moves himself round in the already small space. His whole body fills one side of the shower from the size of him, but he's clearly quite agile as he bends down slightly and in one swoop my legs are up and around his hips, his dick poking into my stomach.

His lips come to my neck, kissing and biting at the sensitive flesh there, moving down towards my collarbone before dipping his head down further, he brings his mouth to my nipple and sucks like his life depends on it. My head falls back as I let out a moan and grind myself against him, getting lost in the moment. "Are you sore this morning baby?" He mutters between kisses, and I somehow utter out a no to him, my brain has drifted off somewhere else, lost in the moment. I'm a little sore but not enough to stop this, but just as quickly as my head floats off somewhere else, I'm soon brought back to the present, when I feel like I've been impaled by his ridiculously hard dick. My eyes widen momentarily as I cry out, feeling him press us against the cool tile of the shower and pushing into me impossibly further than he already is. He picks up the pace quickly, setting into a steady rhythm as I grab onto his shoulders to keep myself from falling.

I feel myself getting to the edge, but I can't quite get myself there, Jaxx picks up on this, upping his pace, as he brings his hand between us, rubbing at my sensitive bundle of nerves, circling a few times and bringing me to climax right along with him. He takes a minute to steady his breathing, holding us in place before he lowers me back down, pressing a kiss to my lips as I try to come down from the high of that intense moment we just shared. Grabbing the sponge from behind me and piling soap on it, he turns to me and begins cleaning me up, paying careful attention between my legs and then moving on to clean himself up.

Once he's satisfied we're both clean he reaches behind me to turn the shower off, opening the door and stepping out to grab the towels, as I step out he opens the towel up for me to walk into and wraps it around my body reaching down and pressing a kiss to my head and I feel myself lean in closer to him. I could get lost in him all over again but I really have to get ready for work, so I reluctantly pull away.

"Are you working today?" I ask looking up to him, he nods to me as he turns to walk back into the bedroom to get dressed, continuing the conversation "Yeah, I'm going to try and find some more information on Liam, and then I'll come back here later, unless you've decided you're going to stay with me". He says it so casually I almost forget we were arguing about this last night, but before I can speak, he turns to look at me with a stern expression on his face "And don't even say what I know you're going to, I will call your brother and tell him, and that will awkward because he doesn't know we are together yet. So pick, your house or mine". I blanch slightly remembering we still need to tell Tristan, but then again, we were meant to be taking things slowly.

"I don't remember having a conversation about us being together Jaxx, and tattling to my brother on me is super childish". I raise a brow at him, crossing my arms over my chest as I wait for his answer. He turns to look at me, seemingly a little hurt by my words, but quickly schools his features, shrugging slightly while answering "I figured after last night it was a bit of a given we are together Grace, but if you'd like a conversation then you can have one.. But I can assure you, conversation or not you're mine and I'm yours, so put whatever label on it you feel comfortable with. This" he says wiggling his finger between the two of us "Is very much exclusive on my end and if you aren't on the same page as me then you tell me now".

Letting out a sigh I perch on the edge of my bed, and Jaxx comes to sit beside me, "I just don't know what to think right now, I've wanted to be with you for so long, but all of this happening right now, is that not making you want to run in the opposite direction?" His arm comes to wrap around my shoulder, pulling me into him as he rests his chin on my head as he sits thinking for a minute.

"I'm not going to go running away because your ex is trying to get back into your life Grace, I meant what I said last night. I love you, and I'll keep telling you that every day until you feel ready to tell me back, I get you might not be there yet and that's okay too, but I'm not going to just give up on you or us because of a few problems along the way. I have resources at my fingertips to help protect you and I'm going to do that, because I can't sit back and watch someone hurt you more than they already have done". His fingers come up to trace along my jaw until they reach my chin where he tips my head up to look at him. "I know it might come across as overprotective and not necessary to you, but it is to me. Just humour me for a couple of weeks and stay with me, or I'll stay here until we know he isn't going to cause you any harm. Please".

I nod to him, giving up the fight because I know he means well, and he's just trying to look out for me, and I'm the one being stubborn by not letting him help. Seeming happy with my non-verbal response he leans down and presses a kiss to my lips, "Good. Right get dressed and I'll go make us some coffee. I'll bring a bag and stay here with you so that you're more comfortable, is that good with you?" I wouldn't win if I said no, and so I smile back at him and nod once more, words lost on me that this man will do anything he can to keep me safe, I just need to learn to accept the help.

After we've had some coffee and I've whipped us up some eggs we head out to our cars and by some miracle, he lets me drive myself to work, which somehow, given our morning together, I've still got five minutes to spare by the time I walk into the building heading straight into the kitchen to make myself a second cup of coffee. I'm sipping away when my phone rings and I look to see my mom calling me.

"Hey mom, are you okay?" She doesn't normally call me up in the mornings but after this past week it's good to hear her voice, "Yes honey, I'm fabulous, I saw my friends yesterday for our sewing class, and Marion mentioned that Alice saw you and Jaxx at the fair together, is there something you forgot to tell me?" I let out a groan letting my head fall into my hand "Ugh mom is there anything this town doesn't know about my personal life. Me and Jaxx .. We.. We're sort of together. It all happened very quickly, and Tristan does not know so don't say anything to him or dad for that matter!!" I rush out my last sentence.

The high pitched squeal of my mom's voice comes through the phone piercing my ears a little and I have to pull it away from my face, wincing at the sheer volume of it, but she's clearly happy about the situation as she starts her rambling, "Oh Grace, this is the best news, you know me and your father were always routing for you two when you were younger and I'm just so happy for you. Please tell me you will both be coming to Sunday lunch this week".

"Mom, breathe. I'll speak to Jaxx and ask him, but remember I just said don't tell Tristan yet. He doesn't know and I want it to come from us". She scoffs down the phone at me "Grace honey, don't worry about your brother, he's a big boy you just do what makes you happy". I let out the breath I didn't realize I was holding, as I smile into my phone. "Thanks mom, I'll see you on Sunday, but I have to get to work right now, so I'll speak to you soon". "Oh no problem sweetheart, I'll see you on Sunday. Love you".

I tell her I love her too and hang up the phone, heading over to my desk and turning on my computer. I go through the few emails that have arrived in my inbox when Jack approaches my desk, he smiles at me and I return one in his direction, "How are you getting on here Grace? Do you need any help with anything?" I look back down to my computer and around my desk, making sure I have everything, before looking back up and replying, "No I think I'm good here Jack, but I will come find you if I need you for anything, thank you though". He gives me a warm smile and knocks on my desk, "Good good, just wave me over if you want me". With that he turns and walks back over to his desk and busies himself with his own work.

I'm working for about an hour when my phone rings and I answer it distracted by my work, "Grace speaking how can I help". I freeze when I hear the voice on the other end. "Grace, It's me Liam. I hope you got my flowers, when are you going to talk come and to me? I know you can't just let us go and I will fight for you. Whatever it takes".

His voice, which I used to be able to listen to for hours on end now just creeps me out, a strange tone lacing it. I sigh into the phone as I try to tamp down the anger I feel bubbling to the surface with this conversation because he won't just take the hint, "Liam we aren't getting back together and you're pretty much stalking me at this point, why can't you just leave me the fuck alone. The police have been told and you need to take the hint. Fuck off". I exaggerate the truth a little because technically Jaxx is the police, but Liam lets out an angry huff down the phone and before I get a chance to hang up, I hear him mutter into the phone "Your mine and the sooner you see that the better".

I slam the phone down into the holder and drop my head into my hands running my fingers through my hair to try and calm my racing heart, but a moment later I feel hands on my back. My head shoots up instantly, panic clawing at me because I just got caught having an argument over the phone whilst at work. A very concerned looking Janet rubs at my back a little more, and let out a small groan, dropping my head again. "I'm sorry if you heard that, my ex is being a weirdo and he's found out where I work and has started calling me, those flowers yesterday were from him too".

She continues to rub soothing circles across my back, "Don't worry about it, it happens to the best of us, but now I know I can help make sure he doesn't disturb you anymore". I give her a small smile, about as much as I'm capable of right now, "Thank you, that means a lot", she smiles back at me and pats my back a little "Don't worry about it dear, how about a fresh cup of coffee and a biscuit?" Taking my cup from me, she heads off to the kitchen whilst I try and figure out how the hell to get Liam to leave me alone.

21

Jaxx

This week has gotten away with me so quickly, that I only realise I've not spoken to Tristan about Grace's assault when she mentions about us going to her parents. I've spent all week at hers as Rose ended up staying away longer and won't be able to get home until the following Tuesday, and Hallie decided to spend an extra week at her brothers, and to be honest I'm not sure I'll be able to go back to not having her around me all the time when they finally come back.

It's Saturday evening and we've just sat down in front of the tv to watch a film for the night, and I'm that lost in thought she clearly thinks I'm upset about her not telling me sooner, "Oh crap I'm sorry Jaxx, it slipped my mind and I didn't even think if you would have had plans, I'll ring my mom now and cancel".

She reaches for her phone and starts searching for her mom's number but I place my hand over hers, so that she looks up at me, "No it's fine I don't have plans, you just reminded me that I haven't yet told your brother about what went on last week, and I'm guessing you haven't either". She looks down, fidgeting with her hands for a minute before sighing and finally looking back up to me, "Jaxx if it's okay with you, I'd rather not tell my family about what happened, I didn't really want to have to tell Rose and Hallie, but since they were there when it happened, I couldn't really avoid it". Part of me doesn't get why she doesn't want people to know, but then I respect her privacy in this situation enough that if she doesn't want to say anything then I'll just drop it.

"Okay that's fine, what about telling him about us? I'm not sure I can keep my hands off you the entire day, and he'll eventually notice me touching you". Her hand comes back over the top of mine, giving it a reassuring squeeze but when I look at her face, it's quite the opposite as she looks back at me with a tight smile instead of her usual relaxed one, "Yeah, we can tell him tomorrow. I've been thinking this week, and I must admit it has been nice spending time with you every day. I know we will have to go back to how it was before when the girls come back, but I do like the idea of us being together properly".

I'm slightly stunned by her sudden decision to make us an official couple, especially since the look on her face doesn't convey the same message as the words that just came out of her mouth, but she quickly smooth's her features, as if this was always the decision she was going to make. Leaning into her, I press a kiss to her lips, "I'd like that very much, I mean to me, you're already mine but I'm glad we're now on the same page". *And soon enough, I'm going to make you my wife too.* I remember not to utter those words out loud to her, knowing it will probably send her in the opposite direction, she's still not said she loves me, and I fucking hope she does soon, but I am not going to pressure her. I mean, I tell her every morning and every night and she just smiles back at me or rewards me with a gentle kiss and I know she's trying to go slow but I can't help myself with her.

……

By the time Sunday afternoon rolls around, I'm getting slightly anxious about the thought of telling Tristan, hoping he will take it well and not lose his shit with me, but I square my shoulders and prepare for the battle ahead, I just don't expect it to be with Grace. Stepping up to the front of the house I go to take Grace's hand in mine, but she pulls back from me, shooting me a guilty look, "Can we wait until my brother knows? I'm just a little nervous that he's going to try and kill you". She lets out a little nervous laugh, and I know she wants to do this on her terms, so I push my disappointment aside and give her a tight smile in return.

Christ, I hope she tells him quickly because I can't go all afternoon like this. I'm lost in my own thoughts as we walk into the kitchen where her whole family are already gathered, but I'm quickly pulled out of them when Tristan starts grilling us, "Why are you two arriving together?" There's a slight accusation in his tone, but I keep my cool and round the counter to say hello to his mom, "Grace came with me" I say as I turn to look at him raising a brow in question "You got a problem with that?" Grace shoots me a look that says don't fucking start and I have to resist the urge to roll my eyes at her. Her mom nudges me a little and when

I look down to her, she's grinning at me with a knowing smile, I guess Grace mentioned something to her then.

He huffs a little, his childlike attitude coming out that he's never gotten rid of, but he quickly recovers, "Yeah, not a problem bro. Just a little odd since you haven't seen each other in so long". I go to tell him that we've actually seen each other plenty, but Grace jumps in trying to cover us up and delaying the inevitable instead of just coming out with it, "He was driving past mine on the way and just offered to drive, no big deal Tristan".

I frown at her but she ignores me, turning away to busy herself with the kids. That was her perfect opportunity to say something then and she avoided it, god this is going to be a long fucking lunch. I walk to the fridge and grab a beer, heading outside so that my annoyance isn't too obvious as I down half my drink in one go, but after a minute outside Lily comes to stand next to me. She's only quiet for a minute before speaking "Just give her a chance, she'll get there, she just doesn't want to upset him".

I turn to her, knowing I can speak my mind with Lily, "I just don't get why she's just blatantly lied to him instead of just coming out with the truth. Could have gotten it over and done with quickly, rip the band aid off". I take another swig of my drink, knowing I better slow down, or I won't be driving later.

Lily shakes her head a little at me "Grace has changed a lot over the last five years. She used to be so outspoken, and say whatever she was thinking, but the last year or so, she's gone in on herself a little. Maybe that just needs to be brought back out of her". My head instantly goes to the thought of what Liam could have been doing to her mentally the whole time they were together, and I have to think carefully so I don't lose my shit "You don't think her ex has had something to do with that do you? He's been messaging her quite a bit and sending her flowers with weird notes on them. I don't want to jump to conclusions, but I'm concerned about her, and now with you saying that, I'm worried that it stretches further than we know".

She waves her hand at me, dismissing the thought, "No I don't think it's that, I think she's just gotten so used to being away from everyone that she doesn't want to upset people by giving them the truth". I'm beginning to think there's more to this situation than I previously thought, but that's pushed to the back of my mind when Brody comes running out to where we're standing to tell us dinner is ready.

We make our way inside, and I'm expecting Grace to be planted as far away from me as possible given the way she's acting, but I'm surprised to find her sitting next to an empty seat. I take up space next to her, shuffling my chair closer to hers as I tuck myself in, and I'm rewarded with a dirty look from her. Oh sweetheart, I'm going to make it so obvious we're together that your brother will have to be blind not to see what's going on.

Maybe he is blind, because he doesn't notice a fucking thing throughout lunch. I kept moving my hand over to her leg, just to have it shoved off again and leaning in close to whisper in her ear. Lily seems to have paid the most attention throughout and keeps laughing to herself, getting weird looks from Tristan, but she brushes it off that it's something Max is doing.

I give up eventually, knowing it's not getting me anywhere and take myself off to the bathroom. I'm about to close the door behind me when it's shoved open, and I'm pushed forward by Grace looking angry as fuck. *Christ* she's sexy like this, I might have to wind her up more often, my dick twitches at the thought.

She's clearly not on the same thought pattern as me though, as she shoves me a little and backs me up to the vanity behind me. "What the fuck was that Jaxx, I told you I would tell him when I'm ready to and you just made it so fucking obvious". I sigh, tipping my head towards the ceiling as I try to gather my thoughts, and when I look back down, her brow is pulled down into an angry frown and she's got her arms crossed under her breasts, pushing them up to give me a nice view of her cleavage. I feel myself get hard looking at her, but she's even more pissed off when she notices where my eyes have wandered too.

"For fucks sake Jaxx, will you answer me. What the fuck are you playing at?" Her tone has my eyes darting up to meet hers, and I narrow them at her slightly, before grabbing her by the waist and spinning us around so that my back is now to the door. It's not locked and anyone could walk in right now, but I don't care because she's getting me riled up with her sassy little attitude.

I lean into her making us eye to eye and keep my voice low. "What I'm playing at Grace, is I don't want to hide what's going on with us from your brother, and the longer you carry this on, the more pissed he's going to be at the both of us, so you need to tell him and tell him soon. You know how I feel about you Grace, but I'm not about to piss him off in the process because you don't want to tell him". I stay in her space, waiting for a reply. Her eyes shifting between mine whilst she has an internal battle with herself in her head.

"This decision isn't up to you and I really don't think you're being fair here". I snort a laugh at her, my patience wearing thin with this conversation, "What's not fair Grace is knowing how badly I want you, and watching you keep our relationship a secret from people, I don't like keeping secrets and you know it".

"Then we don't carry on what we are doing". She says it so casually that I have to rear back as I try to get my head around what she's just said to me, because she's clearly not just heard the words that came out her own fucking mouth. What the fuck is she playing at? I squint at her a little trying to figure her out "What? Why the fuck would we do that? You're not seriously that worried about Tristan, are you? Because I'll go fucking tell him right now". I turn to walk out of the bathroom, but she grabs my arm, her eyes wide with panic, "No don't! Did you not just hear a fucking word I just said to you?"

I cross my arms over my chest staring back down at her "Yeah, I did Grace, and it sounded like you want to call it quits because you're scared of your brother's reaction. You're blowing this way out of proportion and worrying too much about something that probably won't even happen. What's going on?"

She avoids my gaze for a moment, before meeting my eyes trying to act like she can end things that easily, a complete U-turn on everything she said last night, and I'm not going to let her do it to herself or us "You're not going to say anything to him, let me pass, I want to leave". She's acting really odd, so I press her back up against the vanity, my arms coming round to either side of her. "Absolutely not, you're going to tell me what the fuck is going on with you, and you're going to tell me now. You're not going to run away from this conversation".

Her eyes are fixating on a spot on the wall so that she doesn't have to look at me, but I take her chin and pull her face back towards me, "What's gotten you so scared? I need to know so that I can help". Her eyes fill with tears, and she stays quiet for a moment, but she blinks them away, "I'm scared I'm going to lose one of you if we tell him and I don't think I can deal with that. I need to be sure he's going to be okay with us being together".

I still for a moment. She really thinks it will come to that? I wouldn't let that happen anyway, but I need to reassure her. "Baby, you are the most important person to me, and as soon as your brother sees that he will be okay with it. I promise, and if he's not at first then he will come around. You can't put off telling him because it's going to end up being worse if you do".

Leaning in closer to her, I brush my lips over hers trying to convince her that the best option to tell him today, because well it is, and I can't think of any reasons not to tell him. Better to do it sooner rather than later. "What can I do to convince you that this is going to be okay?" She doesn't respond to me because she's so on edge about the whole situation, and the idea pops into my head making me do the only thing I can think of right now that might loosen her up a little and make her relax.

My mouth moves from her lips as I begin to trail kisses down her neck and into the sensitive spot there. She moans into me a little, her hands coming up to grip my shoulders, "Jaxx, don't distract me right now", her words don't match her actions though as she lets out a little moan. *Good.* "Just let me help you relax baby", I say as I slide my hand down into the waistband of her leggings, finding my way to her panties, I slide them to the side and run my finger up and down her slit. She moans a little louder into me, and I cover her mouth with mine to keep her quiet. I might be trying to relax her but I don't need her whole fucking family hearing us.

"Baby you've got to keep quiet, okay?" She nods her response to me and I slip my finger into her, pumping it a few times before I bring it back out, rubbing her wetness over her clit and making small circles over the sensitive bundle of nerves there. I swallow her moans with my mouth as I bring her to the edge more and more, pushing a second finger into her and using my thumb to massage her clit at the same time. She reaches her orgasm quickly, shuddering against me as I keep the motion going whilst she comes back down from her high.

Putting her underwear back in place, I pull my hand out, readjusting the waistband of her leggings as I go and fixing her top. Now she's looking a bit more put together than she was a minute ago, I pull her attention back to me, "Baby, it's going to be fine, you can trust me, we'll go out now and find your brother and tell him together. I don't want to put this off any longer than it needs to be". She finally agrees with me and nods in agreement, "Okay, wait outside for me a minute, I need to use the bathroom, and that's going to be fun when I'm hard as a rock, and I may need a couple of minutes to sort myself out".

She looks down at my pants and laughs to herself before looking back up to me with a cheeky smile on her face, "I could take care of that for you if you like?" She wiggles her brows at me and fuck if that doesn't make my dick ache as it goes impossibly harder. Letting out a groan I close my eyes and give my head a little shake "*Fuck,* baby girl you can definitely help with that later on, but right now I think we should stick to the plan and go tell you're brother". What a mood killer that statement was, but I'm right, that's what we need to do.

She gives me an exaggerated sigh but nods in agreement, "Urgh fine, I'll wait outside". With that she turns to leave the bathroom and I give her a little smack on the ass, "Good girl" I say as I shoot her a wink. She rolls her eyes at me, a little smile creeping up on her lips as she makes her exit and I get to work sorting my little friend out.

22

Grace

By the time Jaxx reappears from the bathroom, I've finally worked up enough courage in my head to tell my brother. I don't even know why I'm panicking so much about it, literally everyone has said he'll be fine, if not now then eventually. I feel a little bad for Jaxx, with me trying to prematurely end things between us, especially after telling him last night that we were moving forward into a new place in our relationship together. Thank god he he's just as stubborn as I am, and amazing for giving me that nice little bathroom pep talk.

He pulls me from my thoughts by putting his arms around me and pressing a kiss to my head, "You alright now sweetheart? It's going to be fine, so please stop worrying" I wrap my arms around him inhaling his scent to calm me, and nod into him. "Yeah, I'm ready to get this over with, I don't know why I'm freaking out so much, but I'll let you take the lead". He pulls back from me slightly, his eyes scanning over my face, making sure I'm really okay with it, and with a firm nod he lets go of me but quickly takes my hand in his, as if trying to stop me from escaping.

I walk down the stairs on shaky legs and into the kitchen where my brother is in deep conversation with Henley, but it stops the minute he spots Jaxx holding my hand, a frown pulls his brows down, and instant panic takes over me as I go to pull my hand from Jaxx, but he just tightens his grip on me. When I look over to him, he just smiles at me and pulls me into him a little more, tugging my hand around so that his front is to my back and his arm crosses over my front, essentially trapping me so I can't escape.

When I look back over to my brother, he's leaning on the kitchen counter, arms crossed in front of him, and one ankle tucked behind the other. His brow is raised waiting for an explanation, and I just want to curl up in a hole, he reminds me of my dad standing like that and I won't lie, I'm not excited for this.

I expect Jaxx to be the first one to speak, but instead it's Tristan, "Anyone wanna explain why the fuck you're touching my sister like that?" The question is asked to us both but clearly directed at Jaxx, I swallow hard trying to keep my cool, but I'm freaking the fuck out. "Tris…." I start but I'm quickly cut off by Jaxx, "We've been seeing each other since Grace got back, and after a few conversations, we have decided that we want to be together. I know it's not what you expected but that's the way it is. I've been in love with her for years and she knows that, we just hope that you can accept this for what it is".

I'm literally cringing as I try to figure out what my brother is thinking. His jaw is clenched, furrowed brow, and he's not saying a word. "I didn't want to upset you, but I want to be with Jaxx, and I really hope that you can accept this for what it is". Tristan is silent for what seems like an eternity, and I expect him to kick off, but instead he just nods his head and says "About fucking time you two admitted your feelings for each other, I was starting to think I imagined it all those years ago, but I'm glad that I was wrong".

Wait *What*? He fucking knew!! Along with my mom dad and sister, they all fucking knew, and I was the only one sitting here thinking I wouldn't ever be able to be with Jaxx! I've been worrying about jack all. It's my turn now to scowl at my brother, he takes one look at me and bursts out laughing. "What the fuck are you laughing at? I've been panicking about telling you this and you're laughing at me?" I feel Jaxx laughing too from the vibration against his chest, and my head swings between the two of them, trying to figure out what the fuck is going on.

"Grace, I've known this whole time there was something between you both, I just couldn't figure out if you had actually been together and that's what caused you to leave. I've had a lot of time to come to terms with this potentially happening and it's okay. Now come here and give me a hug". He opens his arms out to me and Jaxx releases me from his hold, I feel like I'm waiting for the other shoe to drop with this, but when I reach my brother, he wraps me in his arms maybe a little too tight and whispers in my ear, "I am happy for you Grace, I mean, I will definitely kill Jaxx if he ever hurts you, but I have it on pretty good authority that he's a good guy, so I feel alright leaving you in his capable hands". I sigh and collapse into him a little, squeezing him back tighter, "Thank you, you have no idea what's been going through my head this past two weeks whilst I've been waiting to tell you". "I can only imagine, I know you're an over thinker at the best of times, so I don't doubt that this was probably a little bit of torture for you".

I eventually pull back from him, and give him a small smile. He looks over to Jaxx and hikes his thumb over his shoulder towards the back door, "Shall we go for a chat? Promise I won't hurt you... Yet". He's smiling when he says it, but I know my brother, and something tells me he would make good on that promise, even if Jaxx is his best friend.

Jaxx goes to follow him outside, but before he makes it to the back door he stops and pulls me into him, my head against his chest, and kisses the top of my head. "I told you it would be fine baby girl, I'm going to go out there and listen to him give his big brother speech and then I'll be back okay?" I laugh a little and nod into him as he pulls back, gives me a wink and is out the door.

I watch them for a couple of minutes trying to lip read but failing, and eventually give up and go to find my mom and sister in the living room. When I get in there, my mom is sitting on one sofa with my dad, Henley and Lily are sitting on the other, and the kids are playing nicely for a change on the rug. I weave through them and make my way to the winged back chair on the other side of the room, plopping down and sighing loudly whilst shutting my eyes.

"Seems like it went pretty well if you ask me" my sister says from the side of me. I open one eye to peek at her seeing the cheesy grin on her face, clearly amused with herself. "Nah Tris is burying him in the garden as we speak, he thought it was a good act though". I close my eyes again, and my mom lets out a gasp, as if she actually thought I was being serious. "Honey, I don't think she was actually being serious, it was just a joke" my dad says, having to explain our humour to her, "Oh" my mom returns when she finally gets the crap joke I told. Chuckling to myself a little, I open my eyes again looking over to my mom who is scowling at me, "Grace Vale, that was not funny", "It was kinda funny, seeing your reaction" Lily says from across the room. She shakes her head at us as they go back to their conversation from before I came in.

....

It's almost 9pm by the time we get back from my parents, and I'm so ready for bed so we head upstairs and get sorted before climbing in. I snuggle up to Jaxx straight away, glad that we finally got our relationship out in the open with my family, and that I don't have to worry now. "What did my brother say to you before?" I ask. I'd put off asking in the car, because I wanted his full attention on the conversation so he didn't miss anything out.

He squeezes me a little before starting "He basically just said that he's okay with it, maybe not when he first thought years ago but he'd had time to get used to the idea, and then thought it might never happen. So it's been a bit up and down for him, knowing his best friend and his sister might eventually get together, oh and that he'd cut my balls off if I do actually hurt you". I scowl at his bad joke "Why didn't he say something before this then if he thought we might have been seeing each other?" I don't really get why he had never brought it up before. "He said he didn't want to rock the boat with our friendship in case it was actually nothing, but in the end it made things easier for him to process it".

I hum in response to him, "Grace, I promise you everything is going to be fine, you can stop worrying about your brother now because he knows and he is fine with it. We didn't just talk about our relationship but things from our past too, and we are still just as good friends as before. Let's just focus on the now and we can enjoy just being together, okay?" He leans down to press a kiss to my head and squeezes me again.

I let out a sigh, blinking up to him, "I'm sorry I said what I did before about ending things Jaxx, I just panicked". "I know Grace, and for the record, I wouldn't have let you do that either way". I'm lying there thinking for a minute in the darkness, feeling his breathing slow down so I say what I want fast hoping he hasn't fallen asleep. "I know you say it to me all the time and have been waiting for me to say it back, but I want you to know that I do love you too, I've just been waiting until the timing was right to say it". He's so quiet that I decide to peek up to him wondering why he hasn't responded, and I'm slightly gutted to see that he's fallen asleep.

23

Jaxx

Things seemed to have calmed down over the last couple of weeks, Rose and Hallie came back and I was promptly kicked out back to my own place. Grace asked if we could switch between each other's houses a couple of nights a week, and I was more than happy to agree. With me working late some nights, I gave Grace a key to mine and got one to hers in return.

We've settled into our relationship nicely, and Tristan has yet to make good on his promise to cut my balls off if I ever hurt his sister. The only thing that's been bugging me since that day we told him, is that I could have sworn Grace told me she loved me that night, my mind might have been playing tricks on me, as I was half asleep, but she hasn't said it again since. Part of me thinks I imagined it, but she was acting funny around me the next day, so the other part of me thinks she's avoiding telling me again.

Pushing it to the back of my thoughts though, I hit up Luca and Tristan to go out for drinks, and it feels good to have a catch up with my friends again. I feel like we haven't seen enough of each other recently and I'm probably partly to blame for that, having gotten myself far too wrapped up in this whole situation with Liam and I've neglected my friends a little.

Not that they mind at all. Luca is the biggest player I know, with a different girl warming his bed each night, and Tristan keeps himself busy at the ranch with his dad. He's a grumpy bastard at times, but I can usually pull a smile out of him. And tonight, that is very much needed because he's in a bad mood over his parents.

We're all sitting in the local bar Hanks. The owner- you guessed it, Hank, is an older guy who's had this place for the last thirty years, and it's still the best place in town to come for a good night with friends for a couple of quiet drinks. It's a little worn and dated now but it has still got a cosy feel to it. The large brick fireplace in the centre sets the lighting, with old wing-back chairs and wooden tables and a few stools are dotted around the place, and the old carpet that runs through the place could definitely do with being changed soon.

Turning to look at Tristan, who's sat with a face on him, I try get out of him what's got him looking like he just got told the tooth fairy isn't real. "What's up with you man? Not seen you looking this down in a long time". He looks up to me, scowling now, and takes a sip of his drink before answering me, "My parents told me they want me to take over the ranch, dad needs to take a step back and mom wants to travel. They can afford it, but fuck. I don't want them to go, and I know that makes me selfish, but I don't want to be left by myself".

I let out a small laugh glancing over to my friend who scowls harder at me, his blue eyes narrowing in and I can't tell if I should be upset alongside him or carry on taking the piss out of him. “This isn't a laughing situation jackass, I don't think I can run that whole place by myself”. I give him a shrug of my shoulders, watching as Luca joins my side of the discussion. “Sure you can, you hire help and figure it out along the way. Your dad isn't dying, he can pick up the phone and help you if you need it, that place is like a gold mine anyway and with the horses it will be fine”. “Yeah” Luca agrees with me, “You just need to figure out what’s going on. Your sister can help with the financial side of things, why don't you ask her to help run the business alongside you”.

They both turn to me like I'm the one with the answer, but Luca may have just got it spot on. “You know what Luca, that's actually a really good idea, you should talk to Grace about that Tris. I know she's just settled in at the new firm but if she worked with you, then you would have more family around you and not be so lonely”. And I wouldn't have to worry about her so much because I know she'd be safe with her family around.

Tristan is sitting in thought for a moment before turning to me and agreeing with us both, “Yeah, actually I can get on board with that. I think Grace and I will be able to cope with each other and she is good at keeping me on the straight and narrow”. “Well give her a call then and see what she says about it”. He nods his agreement to me, taking another sip of his beer.

He moves in his seat slightly facing Luca and switches the subject onto him. “How’s the new office working out for you then Luca? Slept with your new secretary yet?” Tristan chuckles like it's a joke but we all know Luca has the worst reputation for it. Luca sighs before taking a long sip of his drink and preparing himself for the response "My dad said I should stop hiring women and have a male secretary cause I can't keep it in my pants, can you fucking believe that!" He huffs out his sentence like his dad has said the most ridiculous thing to him, but Tristan and I take one look at each other and burst out laughing. "What the fuck guys, I didn't think you'd both agree with him". He sits back and folds his arms across his chest like a pouty child, making us laugh harder.

I calm my laughter slightly, looking over to him as I give him some home truths, "Luca, your dad's right. Okay, maybe you don't need to settle down right away, but you do need to stop fucking every woman you hire. I know you're a grown ass man and can do what you like, but you're going end up with a sexual harassment lawsuit if you carry it on". He clicks his tongue and rolls his eyes at me, "I'll settle down when I want to, I'm definitely not going to stop fucking who I want though so thank you, but no thanks! And ooft speaking of women, look who's just walked in".

Our heads all turn to look at where Luca is staring to see Grace, Rose and Hallie all appear at the other end of the bar. Tristan waves them over before I even get a chance, as I catch Grace looking slightly shocked to see me but quickly recovers, smoothing her features and giving us a bright smile. She's stunning as usual, her hair tied back in a high ponytail that swings as she walks, dark green parker, and a tight jean clad ass, she looks good. So fucking good. Rose is the first to speak when they approach the table "Hey guys, fancy seeing you here, mind if we join you?" Luca's face couldn't show his interest anymore if he tried, "Sure thing gorgeous, I'm sure we can find a spot for some pretty ladies like you". I smack him around the back of the head at the same time Tristan barks out a laugh, and Rose rolls her eyes at him, "Bro, what the fuck was that for?"

I shake my head at him as Grace moves to stand next to me, "We literally just had a conversation about this exact situation dumbass". He lets out a groan shaking his head, then promptly gets up to get the girls some extra chairs. I don't feel like sitting too far from Grace right now though, so I pull her into my lap. She lets out a little squeal as she falls onto me, and I wrap my arms around her waist, pressing a kiss to her shoulder.

"Right, I'm going to grab another round of drinks, what would you ladies like?" Tristan asks, they all give him their orders and Hallie offers to go with him to help, whilst Rose is sat being eye fucked by Luca, I talk lowly into Grace's ear so we can't be heard. "Why did you just look so surprised to see me then baby girl? Did you not want to see me at all tonight?"

She turns to me slightly so she can see me and talks back quietly, "You know I always want to see you Jaxx, I just wasn't expecting to see you this early in the evening, I was planning on drunk texting you for a booty call later". She winks at me, and I bark out a laugh, causing Rose and Luca's heads to spin in our direction. She waves them off as though it's nothing, but now all I'm thinking about is getting her naked later. My dick is straining in my jeans, and she definitely feels it too because she wiggles her ass about in my lap a little too much, clearly enjoying herself.

I need to get control on the little situation before I fuck her with an audience, and so I grip her a little tighter, holding her in place as I murmur against her ear, “Don't do that unless you want fucking right here Grace, because all my restraint for the evening is quickly leaving my body”. A small giggle leaves her pretty little mouth, as she gives her ass one last wiggle against me, causing me to let out a strangled groan. I cough quickly trying to cover it but Luca clearly spots what’s going on when he smirks over at me. I scowl back at him, and then drop my head onto Grace's shoulder and let out a long breath. She eventually stops moving about so much when her brother comes back to the table, and he looks pointedly at the pair of us. “Could you not have got your own seat to sit on Grace?”

She's clearly more comfortable about the pair of us being around her brother because her sassy little attitude and quick remarks come out for the evening, “Actually Tris, I'm finding this chair rather comfy right now, warming my seat up for later”. She throws him a wink and he scrunches his face up in disgust, “Grace that is too much fucking information, keep it to yourselves, I know I said I was alright with it but fucking hell, I definitely don't need to see it.” She giggles at him waving her hands about, “Oh get over it, I've seen you do and say a hell of a lot worse brother, so I'm sure you can deal with it for one evening”. He grumbles at her in response, and the conversation moves along.

A little while later Tristan and Grace end up talking about their parents and the fact they have decided to retire, and Luca reminds him that he wanted to ask her about a job. “Oh shit yeah, Grace, how do you fancy coming to work with me for the family business?” He gives her his biggest, and brightest grin to try convincing her, but she's not quite sold just yet. “Hmm I don't know if I can handle working with you, you're hard work.” “Amen” Luca butts in, and Tristan scowls over at him in return, “Just have a think about it. Come over to mom and dad’s one night and we can go through everything, I mean I haven't spoken to dad about it yet but I think he will agree too that this is a good idea.

She's quiet for a minute mulling it over, before nodding to her brother. “Okay, I’ll have a run through the financials of the company and get dad to talk me through things, how does that sound? I'm not making any promises though, I need a wage to at least match what I'm on now because I do enjoy my job, and I don't want to leave Rose's dad high and dry so I need to find him a replacement if I do decide to take it. “Don't worry about my dad Grace, I'm sure he will figure something out”. Rose says to her and Grace smiles over at her as Tristan seems to relax a little now that everything is working out in his favour.

We all get into our own little conversations and Grace eventually moves over to where the girls are sitting, swapping places with Luca, he goes to find another chair then comes to sit next to me. “Fuck that red head is a looker”, Luca says eyeing up Rose again. I roll my eyes at him, and Tristan lets out a small laugh at our friend. “Do not even think about it. I've known Rose a long time and you will fucking kill each other”. Tristan says from beside me. Luca hums in agreement, but I keep catching him watching her, so I wait until Tristan is out of ear shot and speak to him “You got a thing for Rose? I have to say I didn't think she'd be your type”. He shoots me a dirty look, but his eyes keep flitting back to her, like he's more interested in the girl's conversation.

Letting out a small sigh he brings his eyes back to me, “She's the furthest thing from my type. I'm usually more attracted to the preppy brunettes I'm constantly spotted with, but there’s just something about her I feel myself being drawn to”. I pat him on the shoulder, “I know buddy, but just be careful with her. She’s not the kinda woman you mess with”. He gives me the side eye, a small smile touching his lips. “Yeah, and therein lies the problem, she’s got a fiery little attitude that I want to fuck right out of her. I chuckle at his comment, shaking my head a little at his delusions. If he wants to think he can get this girl then, he can go for it. I couldn't see that happening in this lifetime.

By the time we’re all heading out, the girls are getting ready to call a cab, so I sneak an arm around Grace before she disappears off with them for the night. “I hope you're coming home with me and not the girls, because I have the day off tomorrow so we can take a long lie in”, she peaks up at me and I wiggle my brows making her giggle as I lean back down to kiss her cheek, “I’m going to take that as a yes baby, go say bye to the girls”, I release her from my hold, and as she goes I give her a little tap on the ass, and I'm rewarded with her sexy smile over her shoulder as she walks away from me.

24

Grace

"Fuck baby, get those clothes off for me, I need you naked".

Jaxx pants out in between kisses, as we barrel through the front door of his house. His hands don't know where they want to go in between each item of clothing coming off and leaving a trail through the house. First my shoes, then his, followed by our shirts and pants, leaving us just in our underwear.

I'm about to turn and climb the stairs, but he grabs me from behind, causing me to let out a little screech as he hauls me up and over his shoulder into a fireman's lift. "Put me down Jaxx" I manage to get out in between bursts of laughter. He slaps me on the ass, marching us into the kitchen where he promptly plops me down on the kitchen island, and slides in between my legs, his hands coming to rest on either side of me on the counter.

His steely grey eyes smooth over me as he brings his face closer to mine, lips almost touching, as he feathers them across my skin before he speaks again. "I think it's a bit far to get up those stairs just yet, and you look good enough to eat right now". I giggle at his comment, placing my arms around his neck and locking my hands there. My head tips to the side as I assess him, and then wrap my legs around his hips to pull him in closer. "I think that's the best idea you've had all night".

His lips twitch a little before they turn up into a sexy smile, as his eyes roam over my face and down to my lacy underwear. He points to them, his fingers coming down to toy with the fabric "These, they need to come off. Now". "Then help me out of them" I return, shimmying a little to give him a little view of the goods. His hands come up and slide round to the back of my bra, undoing it with efficiency, sliding it off my shoulders, and then making his way down to my panties "Lift up" he orders, tapping the sides of my thighs for me to lift my ass off the countertop. I bring my arms down to steady myself, lifting my ass cheeks off the counter so he can slide them down my legs.

He pulls them off my ankles and drops them to the floor, stepping back a little to step out of his boxers, his dick springs up as it comes over the top of them. "Lie back baby, I want to taste you". I do as he says and hiss out a breath as the cool marble touches my skin, my nipples pebbling from the cool sensation underneath me. He continues with his direction "Feet up on the countertop and spread those pretty thighs for me". *Fuck* he can talk to me all night long like that, I feel the heat unfurling inside of me just from his voice alone. I let my knees fall apart slightly, and he comes down to hover over me, his lip darts out skimming his teeth a little. "My favourite view is this right here, you naked and ready for me". His hands come between my legs where he slides two fingers down my slit, coating them, before plunging his fingers inside me and pumping in and out a few times. I moan loudly, my head moving a little from side to side, as I try like hell to keep myself still for him.

It works pretty well until I feel his mouth on me and I gasp at the sudden intrusion. I let out another loud moan, as my hands come up and into his hair where I run my fingers through it, gripping slightly each time he licks me up and down bringing me closer to the edge. “Ahh, fuck Jaxx! Yesss keep going”, I hiss out in between moans. I'm so close to the edge, but he stops abruptly and my eyes shoot open. I’m about to protest when I'm just as quickly dragged to the edge of the counter, he lines himself up and without hesitation, shoves his dick inside me making me cry out at the motion. It doesn't slow him though, as he pumps himself harder into me, and I'm half between crying and moaning his name. Bringing his hand in between the two of us, he rubs circles against my clit bringing me close to the edge again. I feel the tightening in my stomach as I clench my walls, giving him what he needs as I grip him tighter, and I feel myself climax just as he has his own release and spills into me.

We stay like that, panting and trying to catch our breath for a couple of minutes, until he eventually pulls out of me leaving a trail of his seed as it drips down my inner thigh when I sit myself up. His hands come around my back and under my ass as he lifts me into his arms and spins us going toward the stairs. I assume we are going to his room, but he takes us into the bathroom and props me on the vanity whilst he gets the shower ready.

Steam fills the bathroom as he pulls me back off the unit, ushering me inside the shower, grabbing a hold of the sponge and shower gel as he gets to work washing me down. His hands slide over my breasts, and I feel like I could go for round 2 tonight already, but I let him do what he needs to right now. Once he's satisfied that I'm clean he goes to start cleaning himself, but I grab the sponge from him "My turn" I say raising my brow at him. He lets out a little sigh but allows me to do what I want anyway, hands dropped at his sides, keeping his restraint in tact. I work my way down his body with the soap, washing it off as I go, until I find my way to his dick, where I use my hand instead of the sponge to clean him down.

I drop the sponge to my side and take him in my hand, just about able wrap my fingers around his length, stroking him a few times, and taking him from semi hard to full blown erection. I pump him a few more times, and then drop to my knees. "Grace, what are you doing?" Jaxx asks from above me. I look up to see him, clenched jaw, furrowed brow like he has no clue what I'm about to do. I roll my eyes at him and look back at his dick licking my lips. "Getting a taste of you for a change, what does it look like?" "You don't have to do that, I enjoy tasting you, but I'm quite alright if you don't...".

I look back up to him, brow raised at his statement. "Jaxx, shut up and let me enjoy myself for a moment please". He lets out a low chuckle, shaking his head at me "Brat" he murmurs under his breath, before grabbing my ponytail and wrapping it around his hand a couple of times. "Open up and take me then, before I fuck the attitude right out of that pretty mouth of yours". He nudges his dick towards my mouth, and I gladly open up taking him in. My tongue slides along the bottom of it sliding it in and out, before letting it go with a loud pop. I keep my hand on the base of it as he guides me back onto him again.

When I peek up at him, His head is tipped towards the bathroom ceiling, jaw tight and fist clenched at his side. His stomach sucks in as I take him further down my throat, bobbing his dick in and out of my mouth. It doesn't take him long after that, but as he's about to have his release he tries to pull back from me, "Grace, I'm close baby, so stop or it's going straight down your throat". That pushes me to the finishing line quicker, as I grip him a little tighter, my free hand reaching round to grab his ass as I suck his dick like my life depends on it. He lets out a loud moan a moment or two later, as I feel saltiness from him shooting into my mouth and down my throat.

His breathing becomes choppy as I release him, but he helps me up quickly. Pulling me closer, he presses a kiss to my lips, tasting himself on me and smiling against my lips. "That was the best fucking blow job I think I've ever had, but now I want you again". I giggle back to him, and we quickly shut off the shower and pull each other back into the bedroom and onto the bed, making it wet but too in the moment to care.

He pulls himself up the bed towards the headboard, dragging me with him and pulling me to straddle him. My hair has come out of my hair tie slightly, and his hand comes up to tuck a few loose pieces behind my ear. “Sit on it baby”. Don't need to tell me twice. I lift myself up, his hands gripping my hips as I slide myself onto his length, “Ohh, shit that’s so good”, I manage to get out as I rock my hips into him a little and gain friction off him. He pulls my head towards him and his lips come crashing down on mine. We're quick and lost in the moment, but I finally blurt out the words I've been waiting for the right time to tell him. “I love you Jaxx, I really do”. He stills for a moment as his eyes come up to meet mine, shock plastered across his face.

After what feels like forever, the shock must wear off because the biggest grin spreads across his face, and he grabs me pulling my face into his big hands and plants kisses on my lips. He quickly flips us so I'm underneath him planting more kisses across my face and neck, “Fuck Grace, I feel like I've been waiting forever to hear you say that, I love you too baby girl. You're mine and always have been, and I'm never letting you go, you got that?” I nod back, smiling back at him, and he growls against my lips, “Words Grace, now would be a great time for you to use them. Tell me your mine baby”. His dick finds its way into me again and he pumps slowly waiting for me to reply to him, “I’m yours”, I pant out between moans, making his smile widen at me, “That’s right, you're mine and that’s the way it's staying forever. And one day, hopefully in the near future I'm going to make you my wife and the mother of my children too. I've waited too long for you and I won’t let you go again Grace”.

My heart fills with warmth at his words, because *fuck* I want that too. I smile back up to him as I reply “Mmm hmm, I think I can agree to that, let's just get as much practice in as we can before then hmm?” “Fuck yeah, baby. You can have all the practice you like”. He picks up the pace after that giving me another orgasm, and we lay together catching our breathe before he climbs off the bed and goes to grab a washcloth from the bathroom to clean me up again.

When he climbs back into bed he pulls me to him, one arm under my head, the other making lazy circles up and down my arm. My head rests on his chest as I drift off to sleep, and I picture how perfect our life could be together.

25

Grace

I'm seriously starting to regret agreeing to meet with my brother to discuss a business plan for us to work together when mom and dad retire. I agreed last week to come here and meet with him and my dad, and now I feel as if I've just wasted an entire Saturday afternoon listening to him waffle a load of crap. He's been going over the same shit for the last hour, basically explaining that he'll be in charge of the whole business, and I'm going to lose my shit with him if he doesn't let me get a word in. My dad's sitting in his office chair, and my brother and I are opposite him trying to go through what we would need to sort out the running of the business side of things once they go off on their travels.

I let out a huff slamming down the paperwork on the desk a little too hard, "Right that's it! I can't do this anymore, you are going to fucking drive me insane if I work with you, because right now you're trying to make it sound like this is your business". He looks at me with a stoic expression, like he doesn't actually give a shit about my opinion either way. "Grace, I'm going to be running the day-to-day stuff. You're just going to be handling the finances, so I don't really get what the issue is". I blink back at my brother, "Then why they fuck did you advertise this like we were going into business together. I'm not fucking working for my brother, never in this lifetime will I do that".

He scoffs at me and is about to reply but my dad cuts in first, "What Grace is trying to say Tristan, is that she wants more responsibility and a bigger part in the decision-making side of things, and to be honest, I'm thinking that this could be a good idea. It would be less stressful for you, and you can work on the manual side of things more.

He rolls his eyes at my dad and sits back in the chair, arms folded across his chest, with a pouty expression on his face like a petulant child. "I'm perfectly capable of running more than just the horse side of things dad, she's not even been back in town five minutes and you're practically passing the business over to her". I feel my anger rising toward my brother, "You literally fucking brought it up, and that's the only reason I'm sat here right now. So I either take more responsibility or you do it all by yourself, your choice". Fuck me I need a drink after this.

He sits mulling it over for another minute before he eventually relents and allows me to have more access to the decision making, and since my dad is fully on board, we eventually decide that we should get things going as soon as possible.

I say my goodbyes to my dad and brother and pop over to the house to see my mom and sister quickly before heading to get groceries. Sticking my head into the kitchen, they're both sitting gossiping with a cup of tea in hand. My mom spots me first and jumps up,

“Grace, do you want a cup of tea before you get off?” I shake my head a little, giving her a soft smile, “I wish I could, but I have to get to the store before it closes, I just popped in to say bye before leaving”.

“Did you have fun with dad and Tristan there then?” My sister says smirking at me from over her cup. “I did, I've already decided where I'm burying Tristan so it’s all in hand”. She laughs at me but my mom scowls, “Grace it can't have been that bad, and Lily why weren't you in that meeting, this business is just as much yours as it theirs you know”. Lily looks over to mom, a bored expression on her face, “Mom I have four babies to watch and running a business is the least of my priorities right now, plus Henley has a good job, we don’t need the money.”

Mom scoffs at her but I get where Lily is coming from. She never wanted a career, she always wanted to be a mom and Henley is amazing and supports that by providing for their family. “Anyway, I’ll catch up with you both some other time, I've got to shoot”. I wave my goodbyes to them, and head out front to my car, trying to put a mental shopping list together in my head before I get to the grocery store.

I'm wandering around in my own world, not noticing a damn thing that’s going on around me, when I'm startled by a hand grabbing my upper arm. I suck in a sharp breath as I turn around and come face to face with Liam, my face quickly turning from shock to anger, as I yank my arm out of his hold before spinning on him to face him.

“What the fuck are you doing here Liam and why are you following me. I’m not in the mood for your shit today". I go to walk away from him again, but he stops me by stepping in my way and getting in my face a little. "You won't answer my fucking calls Grace, what was I supposed to do?" I feel my anger taking over as I turn my gaze up to meet his, I need this conversation over with now "Take the hint and leave me alone. I don't want you following me around, and the fact I haven't been taking your calls is because I blocked your number so you can't contact me anymore, how hard is that for you to understand?" I shift myself to move away from him, but he blocks my path once more.

"I Told you Grace, you're coming back home with me, I made a mistake, and we need to sort things out. So, I'll take you back to your friend's house and you can grab some of your things until we get you settled at home". I rear back at him, is this guy for fucking real. "I'm with someone else now Liam, there is no us and the sooner you realise that the better. You wasted your time coming all the way here, because I have nothing else to say to you".

He grabs my arm tightly and gets in my face a little more, anger evident on his features as he backs me against one of the shelves, "You've made a big mistake here Grace, and if you think this is over then you think again". He pushes me a little as he lets me go, causing a couple of the tins behind me to fall off the shelf.

My hand comes up to my chest as my pulse beings to race, and I crouch down to the floor trying to get my breathing back to normal. I can't help it as I start hyperventilating, my breathing refusing to return to normal anytime soon. Just then a staff member rounds the corner and sees what's happening, she comes over and crouches beside me “You're okay, just breathe, I think you're having a panic attack”.

She keeps repeating the same words to me until my breathing returns to normal, once I feel like I can stand again and I feel like I'm more myself I turn to her, “Thank you so much for that. I don't know what happened there”. She looks around quickly, scanning the store to make sure we're out of earshot from anyone before returning her gaze to me “I saw that guy bothering you and wanted to check on you. He stormed out quickly and when I found you and saw what state you were in, I just wanted to make sure you were okay”. I smile back at her and nod, trying to reassure myself as well. “Yeah, I’m good, just a little shaken up by him. Please don’t mention what you’ve seen to anyone though, he's just my ex being a bother and I don't want to worry anyone”.

The lady eyes me sceptically but eventually nods to me, and I get the rest of the bits I need now I've calmed myself down a little. I make it back to the house checking everywhere as I go along, and once inside I bolt the door shut. Rose and Hallie are both away for the weekend and Jaxx is working late, so the last thing I need is him worrying about me whilst he’s on shift.

I close all the curtains, grab a bottle of wine and my book and head up to my bedroom. Where I finally manage to relax a little bit, losing myself in the story.

•••••

I'm woken to the feeling of something grabbing a hold of my waist, panic claws up me as I start screaming, trying to get out of the grasp of strong arms. I'm pulled backwards and the fear escalates to a new level. *Shit he's got me,* I think to myself as I scream more pulling away from him, but I'm pinned down on the bed. "Shhh Grace, It's me. It's just me, you're okay baby". I'm still trying to escape him, thrashing around in the bed when he speaks more firmly to me, shocking me out of my nightmare, "Grace! Stop, its me, Jaxx". I take a breath from screaming and crying, realising I recognise the voice. His arms come around me and pull me up to him, cradling me and pulling me in to cuddle hold me closer. "Shh baby, I've got you".

I lose it as a sob wracks through my body, I shake as I cry uncontrollably into him. I don't want him to know what's happened today, but I also don't know how I can keep this up, fighting against Liam. "What happened baby? Did you have a bad dream?" I decide to avoid the truth for now and just nod into him, hoping that I can figure this out by myself in the meantime. "I'm sorry baby, wanna talk about it?" I shake my head, not trusting my voice right now. "Okay, that's fine, I'll just sit with you a minute, I'm sorry I didn't mean to startle you, I got in late and just climbed straight into bed".

I take in a deep breath, calming myself as much as I can before responding to him, "It's okay, I just forgot you were coming over tonight and with that and the bad dream it caught me off guard". It was only a white lie, I was playing the nightmare in my head over and over again on repeat, and him touching me brought back the memory from Liam grabbing me earlier today.

He tucks us in under the covers, holding me through my tears as he tries to console me. After a little while my breathing finally calms and I fall into a deep dreamless sleep, the bad dreams temporarily forgotten.

26

Jaxx

"You got me anything on Liam Fennel yet?" I ask with a clipped tone into the phone, I'm trying to be patient with Harris, because I know he's literally the best at what he does, but I'm losing that patience very quickly. The more the days drag on into weeks, it's sending me insane because I can't get any more info on the guy and it's driving me up the wall. I know he's taking things up a notch stalking Grace, because one of my guys said they spotted his car a few days ago.

The same night Grace woke up terrified when I climbed into bed with her. She wouldn't tell me what had gone on, but I know he's shaken her up more this time. He seems like the dullest guy on the planet on paper, but I have a feeling that was just a facade to other people, maybe even Grace.

"Well, hello to you too Jaxx.. You'll be very happy to know that I do actually", he says it so cheerfully down the phone that I'm suddenly very hopeful for this conversation. "Hit me with it". I reply, trying to keep myself from getting too excited about this, because it could very well be another dead end, but a little hope never hurt anyone. He's quiet for a second whilst he shuffles papers round and taps away on his computer, "Right, so he got fired from his job about a week and a half ago, and he's been spotted in town a couple of times. I know he's sitting on quite a bit of cash, so he's not going to struggle paying his bills for a while, but he has been at this job since he turned eighteen. He seemed to have been working his way up the business, so it doesn't quite add up that he would just get fired".

"Hmm yeah, that is odd. But then if he wasn't expecting his relationship to end then that could have rocked the boat for him at work, maybe because he's been showing up in town so much, he'd have had to take some time off work or something and they didn't like it, I know Grace said in the past to her brother that he never took vacation days". I ramble on down the phone, nerves getting the better of me, as I voice my thoughts to him. He's quiet for a moment, but I can hear background noise, so I know he's still there.

"Yeah, that's possible too, I'm going to look more into his financials and maybe past relationships before Grace, see if there's anything I can spot there, leave it with me and I'll get back to you". *Great,* more waiting. "Alright, thanks Harris. Let me know as soon as you can, bye".

Once I hang up on him, I get to work seeing if I can delve into any criminal background checks that I might have missed, and to my surprise a couple of warnings were issued against him, but nothing ever came from them. Maybe that's why they hadn't shown up previously. When I check into what the warnings were for, I'm not surprised in the slightest to see they are, in fact, warnings for harassing his two previous ex partners, something I should have spotted sooner.

I have an internal debate for a little while as to whether or not I should tell Grace, but I don't want to worry her any more than she already seems to be. I figure I should keep it to myself for a little while, but the need to tell her brother compels me as he's the next best person who can help me with this, finding his name in my phone, I'm only waiting for a couple of rings before Tristan answers.

"Hey Jaxx, You okay man?" He sounds a little out of breath, and I'm assuming I've caught him in the middle of his workday. I try to think of the easiest way to tell him, but there really is no soft landing to explain that your girlfriend's ex is stalking her.

"Erm no not really, look I need to talk to you about something that I probably shouldn't be telling you. Grace will kill me if she finds out, but before I say anything, I need to know you can keep this to yourself". He huffs down the phone, clearly not liking the way I've gone about asking him to keep his mouth shut. "Spit it out Jaxx, is my sister in some sort of trouble?"

I play with the pen on my desk, rolling it up and down whilst trying to come up with the best answer, I sigh down the phone before telling Tristan what's going on, "Yeah, you could sort of say that, but it's not something she's done. Look there's no easy way to say this so I'll just come out with it. Liam is stalking you sister, and she could be in some serious danger, but she keeps brushing it off as if it's nothing and I'm not so convinced that he's harmless". "Fuck" Tristan murmurs down the phone, more to himself than me. I panic a little when he goes quiet, knowing he's probably trying to figure out how he can fix the situation, "You can't go raging into this like a fucking bull in a China shop either, she thinks its nothing and if we bombard her with this, she won't tell me anything else, I think he's already paid her a visit and she hid that from me. The last thing I want right now is to push her away. I've only told you, because I need to know what you know about him, anything that Grace might have mentioned before?"

"Fuck Jaxx, this isn't something small. *Shit* I don't know how to keep my cool in this situation right now" Tristan snaps down the phone, I get he's pissed. Hell, I am too, but I need him to sort his head out and help me right now. "Tris, I know this isn't the conversation you were hoping for on a Wednesday afternoon, but that's the situation, so pull your head out your ass and think for a second".

He's quiet for so long, I almost think he's hung up on me, but eventually he gives me a little bit of information. "I know he has a bit of a temper; Grace was left crying once when he stormed off after a family party. I told her to dump his ass then, but she said it was fine. I don't think he's ever hit her though, just all mouth. I'd have buried him a long time ago if I ever thought he had even hurt her physically. He texted her a lot when she came back by herself too, like he needed reassurance that she was going back home to him".

"Yeah, I'm getting the impression that Grace swept a lot under the rug, and maybe even had rose tinted glasses on for their entire relationship. *Jesus* this is going to be a fucking nightmare getting him to leave her alone. I'm going to have to try and put some sort of restraining order put against him, can you think of anything else that might help me?"

He's quiet for another moment, wracking his brain for any more information, "No that's all I can think of right now, but I'll let you know if I think of anything else". I'm about to hang up when he speaks again, "And Jaxx, make sure you do everything you can to look after her. She's my baby sister, I need her to be safe". I sigh into the phone again, "Yeah Tris I know, I need her safe too, speak to you soon."

He hangs up and I drop the phone onto the desk, scrubbing my hands over my face as I let out a groan. Fucks sake. Why can nothing just be plain sailing for once in my life.

I only sit in my thoughts for a minute when my phone rings again, I see my mom calling me and I think better of ignoring it, because I've been avoiding her since she was rude to Grace at my place the other week. "Hey mom, how are you?" I barely get my words out before she starts, "Don't give me that tone, Jaxx. You haven't called me in nearly a month, and you think I'm going to be okay", she screeches her reply into the phone, and I begin to regret answering the call all together. "You do know that phone calls work both ways mom, you could have called me too, but I've been busy, so I'm sorry for that, but I have time to talk to you now, so I'll try again. How are you mom?"

She huffs into the phone, like I'm the one being difficult before finally replying to me "I'm fine, thank you for asking, I went to lunch with a couple of friends the other day, and one of the ladies mentioned that you and Grace are now seeing each other, I did figure that anyway, but it would have been nice to have the conversation with you about it first".

I drop my head into my free hand, rubbing my fingers across my forehead and hoping it will stop the oncoming headache I can feel rapidly progressing the longer this conversation continues. "Mom I'm sorry, the last few weeks have been a lot, there's been lots of things going on that I can't really talk about with you right now".

"Oh god, you haven't got her pregnant already have you?" My head drops back onto my chair, as I shut my eyes groaning into the phone, this fucking woman.

"Fuck's sake mom, no. Grace isn't pregnant, how the hell did you even.. you know what, never mind it doesn't matter. Look I have some important things at work that need my attention, can I talk to you some other time?" She huffs out a fine to me and then ends the call.

Christ that was just too much to deal with for one day, and now all I can think about is actually getting her pregnant for real. I just need to sort this fucker out first.

27

Grace

Friday nights are the new wine and catch-up nights in our house. It's 8pm and Hallie, Rose and I are currently all lounging on the sofas whilst we're waiting for our pizza delivery to arrive, cosying up in our fluffiest pyjamas, we've all got a glass of overfilled sauvignon in our hands. I'm sitting up on the sofa leaning against the arm rest, legs crossed at the ankle, watching Rose as she tells us about her new contract at her job. The ice clinks around in her glass as she talks to us, moving her hands around far too much with all the animated talking.

Whilst Rose talks, my mind wanders off to my own work and the stalking with Liam. I have been trying to decide all week if I should spill the beans about him, but I'm trying not to worry myself over it. It escalated more today though when I spotted that car again, waiting outside the deli. He hasn't approached me again since last week, but I know he's watching me. I never thought about this possessive side to him a lot when I was with him, but now that I'm witnessing this first hand, it's making me realise all the signs I clearly chose to ignore when we were together. All the times he would call to check where I was, playing it off saying he was making sure I was safe.

All the texting when I'd come back to visit my family without him, it was way more than necessary but I never thought about it at the time. He'd always follow up a message with how much he missed me or that he loves me, and he'd sweet talk me into thinking everything was normal, and keep me on the phone tracker, so he knew I was 'safe'.

Fuck. Only now am I starting to realise that this was his whole personality all along and he'd hidden it from me. Or I was just to blind to see it, but either way I know I need to nip this in the bud and soon.

I'm pulled from my thoughts by Hallie, when she nudges my arm a little causing the ice to clink in my own glass. I look down at it then back up at her, she's got her brow raised at me and I realise I've just been caught not paying any attention. God I'm such a shit friend at the minute. My eyes flit in Rose's direction who has yet to even notice I'm not listening, and I side eye Hallie when she shakes her head at me. "So basically, I've got to go back to Seattle again from tomorrow afternoon, and I'll probably be gone for about a month. I should be back just before thanksgiving". *Wait what?* My mouth pops open as I gawp at my friend "You're going to be gone for a whole month?" I turn to Hallie "And you're going back to your brothers for another 2 weeks?" they both nod at me, and I realise I might be slightly screwed because I don't want to stay alone right now.

Hallie's brother Hunter lost his wife shortly after their little boy was born, and so she's been back and forth helping out as much as she can, I feel bad for wanting her here with me, but I also feel like I can't voice that right now, without telling them about the Liam situation getting worse. Hallie reaches over and pats me on the leg reassuringly, “Don't worry, you'll be fine. I’m sure Jaxx can stay with you for a few nights extra if you don't want to be alone all the time”. I shake my head to clear my thoughts a little, trying not to show the anxiety taking over me right now “No it's not that, well it kind of is”. Letting out a sigh, I fall back into the sofa a little, making my wine slosh around in my glass. I look down at it whilst I speak because I find the whole situation utterly embarrassing, and well they deserve to know the truth.

“I… He... Ugh, Liam has been following me and sending things to my work. I thought it was just harmless at first, but then he cornered me last week in the grocery store, and I panicked. He got a little aggressive but then seemed to leave it at that. Then I saw his car outside the deli again today at work, and now I'm freaking out a little”.

Rose is up and out of her chair immediately, walking over and squashing herself on the sofa with Hallie and me. “Grace, why the fuck have you waited this long to say something to us? He's clearly unstable if he's following you around. I'll stay home and cancel the job; your safety is more important, and I don't want you here by yourself when he’s lurking around”. My eyes go wide as saucers, and all the colour drains from my face as I look over to my selfless best friend. Hallie butts in then too, “No don't be silly Rose, I'll stay behind with her, I'm sure Hunter won't mind”. I blink back at the two of them, a firm resolve in my voice as I say, “No there’s no chance in hell that you two are going to put off what you need to babysit me. I'll be fine and I'll see if Jaxx will come stay for a while, or I can go to his place". I shrug my shoulders trying to act as casual about the situation as possible, but I'm inwardly panicking a little at the thought of what might happen if I'm left by myself.

They're both looking at me, sceptical still and clearly not convinced that I can somehow keep myself safe. I wave them off bringing my drink to my mouth, talking before I take a sip, "Honestly girls, I'll be furious with the pair of you if you even think of cancelling your plans to stay with me. I'll make sure to lock the doors and I'll go to my mom and dad's any time if I need to, so stop looking at me like that, the pair of you" I say as my finger comes up wiggling it between the two of them.

Rose rolls her eyes at me, whilst Hallie's narrow in on me, trying to assess if I'm going to be okay whilst she's gone. I squint back at her, trying to imitate the serious look on her face and lighten the mood a little, it must work because she lets out a little cackle, shaking her head as she gulps down the last bit of wine in her glass, before giving me a pointed look, "If there are any problems at all Grace, you call me straight away. I can get here quicker than Rose, so just call and I'll be here asap. Okay?" I nod at her before downing the rest of my drink too, the doorbell goes then so Rose jumps up to get the pizzas.

I collect their glasses up and head over to the fridge to do us all a refill, and when I look out of the window, I swear I see someone move across the back yard. But as soon as the thought enters my head, I push it straight back out, it must have been the trees picking up in the wind or something. My mind is starting to play tricks on me, and I need to stay as calm as possible if I'm going to manage here by myself for at least two weeks.

28

Grace

I manage a whole week, almost by myself. Jaxx comes to stay a couple of nights and then we swap, and I go to his, it's worked out well for us all week and to be honest, I'm quite enjoying him demanding he stay close. But now It's Saturday evening again, and it's also Halloween. I've gone all out and decorated the house for the trick or treating later on, a bowl of candy is sitting by the front door, and I've lit just about every candle I can find in the house, giving it the cosy Halloween vibe I'm going for.

I grab a bottle of wine out of the fridge and leftovers from last night, to settle on the sofa and have a dinner date with my new book. Jaxx is having to work late tonight with it being the one day of the year that kids decide to play up and decorate people's houses with eggs and loo roll. The door goes almost every couple of minutes with kids in all various costumes, and by the time 9pm rolls around I'm out of everything I have to give them.

The door goes again, and I shout out to it, "We're out of candy now, sorry kiddo's", hoping that will be enough to send them away. *They should be in friggin 'bed now surely.* But then the door goes again a couple of times in a row, and whoever is at the door is clearly impatient for their non-existent candy, “All right, all right. I'm comin, hold your horses will ya”.

I swing the door open, expecting to find a group of kids waiting on the other side. But instead, my blood runs cold. There stands Liam, his once-sparkling blue eyes now hollow, with a dark, sinister expression twisting his face.

“Trick or treat, Grace”.

29

Grace

"Trick or treat, Grace".

I stumble back a little, my mind in a fog as I try to figure out what the hell he's doing here, but I realise a second too late that I'm giving him space to walk into my home. Trying to fumble my way back to the front door I grab it, pushing against it as quick as I can but not quick enough as Liam pushes his way into the house, closing the door behind him. I square my shoulders, clearly trying to sound braver than I feel, "Get the fuck out now Liam. I don't want you here and you're not welcome".

He shakes his head, clicking his tongue at me, whilst taking slow and meaningful steps towards me. "Grace, how many times are you going to keep pushing me away before you realise, I'm always going to come back for you, I missed you, you know, and I wanted to make this work between us but then I thought about how you so easily threw us away and I have to say I'm really not happy about it". I scoff at him, trying my hardest to keep my distance, but each step I take backwards, he takes another forward, closing the distance between us.

"Liam, you are the one who ruined things, you're the one who cheated. Not me. You." I point at him as if trying to make my point more clear, all he does is look at my finger before he looks back up to me with a blank expressions as he continues to take his slow and practised steps forward. "You know Grace, I probably would have forgiven you for leaving me, and we could have worked through things, but then you had to go ruin it and tell me you were seeing someone else so soon after you left, tsk, tsk. Bad move Grace".

I bump into the wall leading to the kitchen as I continue the walk backwards, my voice coming out wobbly as I try to speak, "N.. no. You don't get to do that. You can't expect me to stick around after what you have done. I can't be with you Liam. I won't"

He stops for a moment, his hollow eyes coming to meet mine once more. "I thought for a while about what would happen when I came here for you. You seem to disappoint me at every turn Grace, you just don't seem to understand, if I don't get you, then no one does".

I don't even have time to think before he jumps towards me, arms reaching out to grab me, and I try to turn and run but the second I do, he grabs a hold of my hair yanking me backwards into him. Pain rips through my head as it's pulled back tightly against him, his free hand coming up to wrap around my neck, squeezing it a little, his breath fanning my cheek as he leans in to speak to me "Don't run from me Grace, it will just make it worse for you in the end".

Fear grips me and I momentarily freeze, trying to figure out what my next steps can be. I do the first thing that comes into my head as I slam my fist backwards into his balls hard, pushing myself off him at the same time. He lets out a grunt, his hands loosening long enough that I can scramble away "You fucking bitch. You're gonna pay for that" I hear him cry out as I make a run for the stairs.

I make it to the bathroom in my room, turning every light on in the house as I go to try and confuse him as much as possible. locking myself in quickly as I rush to pull my phone from my pocket. I hit the floor and move to the other side of the room as fast as my legs allow, struggling through tears to get my phone open. I know I can't ring Jaxx because Liam will hear me on the phone. I send off a text in the hopes that he looks at his phone quickly.

Me: SOS!!!!! EMERGENCY AT THE HOUSE. LIAM IS HERE AND TRYING TO GET ME!!! PLEASE COME QUICKLY!!!

I send a silent prayer that Jaxx isn't called out on a job and is in fact looking at his phone. Just as I press send though, Liam begins banging on the bathroom door and trying the lock. "Grace, open this fucking door now, or so help me I will fucking break it down". He pounds on the door, trying to break it in as silent tears run down my cheeks, I bite down on my fist to try and muffle the sounds of my crying. I know he knows I'm in here, and it's only a matter of time before he finally reaches me.

Looking down to check my phone again, the message comes up as undelivered, *fuck* why isn't it sending. I try again and it does the same. Why the fuck is my phone not working!! I turn the flight mode on and off again, and realise I have no signal whilst I'm trapped here in the bathroom, realising I need to get at least into my bedroom for it to send.

The banging goes quiet for a few minutes, and I think he might have given up trying to get to me, but the silence is soon interrupted when I hear something heavy thud against the door. It carries on until the wood starts to give way, and Liam eventually makes his way into the room.

I scramble to my feet as quickly as I can, tucking my phone into my shorts so he can't see it. The door splintering a moment later and I come face to face once more with a furious looking Liam, he's glaring at me, red faced and chest heaving from the exertion of him throwing himself at my door. I scream as I try to run past him, because this is a fucking horror movie and not my god dam life right now. Surely this can't be real, on Halloween of all nights. *Fuck my life.* If I ever make it out of here alive, I'm never going to take Jaxx wanting to protect me for granted ever again.

My efforts are in vain though as I'm clearly not fast enough because he grabs me, pushing me hard against the door frame, smacking my head off the side of it as he does. I begin to see stars as my vision blurs a little, before coming back into focus. “Don't fucking try to run from me again Grace, or I promise I'll make this drag out even longer for you”. I don't listen to him though, and clearly think I can fight him because, get on my tiptoes as he turns his head for a split second and head but him.

He stumbles back slightly, giving me a split second to make a run for it, I dart from my room and am halfway to the stairs when I see him appear in the doorway, so I turn and try to go quicker, but as I reach the last few steps, I lose my footing and trip, falling and hurting my ankle on the way down. Pain shoots through my leg as I try to stand again, and it takes a couple of seconds too long for me allowing him to reach me.

Grabbing me roughly he pulls me up a little and punches me in the face, causing my vision to blur once more. I fall to the floor, blood seeping from my nose where he's hit me. He comes down to my level and gets up close in my face. "I fucking told you not to run, but I will tell you now, I wasn't joking when I told you that if I don't have you no one else ever will, and I will personally make sure of it". He stands then, kicking me so hard that I keel over winded and begin coughing. "Please," I manage to whisper, my voice barely holding steady. "Why are you doing this, just leave me alone and move on with your life". I cough some more trying to get what little air I can into my lungs, but just as I do, he kicks me again, this time grabbing at my hair, and pulling my face back to look him in the eyes. "I was never going to be enough for you, was I Grace? You were always going to leave me eventually, so this is the only way I get to keep you locked in my memory".

My mouth drops open at his brutality, "You're sick Liam, can you not see that. You don't deserve to be happy if this is the way you treat people". He gives me a bored look, clearly done with the conversation. I think he might actually leave me alone for a moment, but its short lived, when the grip on my hair tightens again, and I'm dragged back up onto my feet, he pulls me along by the hair until we are in the living room where he throws me down to the floor, but as I go, I hit my head hard on the coffee table.

I know at that moment I am about to pass out, as I feel the consciousness drain from my body, and he clearly sees that as his lips form into a cruel smile. I no longer have the energy to fight him, so I just lay there looking at him while the life seeps out of me.

Crouching down to my level, he kisses me on the forehead before leaning in close to my ear. "Good-bye Grace, I'll miss you". A silent tear streaks down my face as I watch him stand again and walk over to the candles by the window, moving them close enough to the curtain that they quickly catch fire. The bastard is actually going to kill me and make it look like an accident. Panic consumes me as smoke begins filling the room slowly, and I try not to inhale it, but I feel it seeping deep into my lungs bit by bit.

He takes one last look at me, blows me a kiss and then makes his exit out of the back door, just as the darkness consumes me.

30

Jaxx

“I think it's gonna be a busy one tonight” I say, letting out a sigh, I grip the steering wheel a little tighter as I look over to Mike, who shakes his head back at me while his eyes focus in on the bar where it's just starting to get a little more crowded for the evening. “Yeah, I think you might be right there”. It's Saturday night and Halloween rolled into one night, the worst combination if you ask me. The local town is crawling with half-dressed females, and men covering their faces in masks, but making no effort with the rest of their outfits.

I look down to my watch and stifle a groan as I realise it's only 9pm, knowing we're going to be in for a long night. We're driving around in the car for a little while making half-hearted conversation, then I remember about the case he was working on the other week. “Hey, did you find out where that young girl came from in the end?” He looks over to me letting out a chuckle as he shakes his head. “Yeah, turns out she was lying about her name, and when we finally dug deep enough, she came from a family up in the north, her mom has been looking for her for weeks.

I shake my head at how easily these kids seem to be able to just run away from home, “Jesus, these fucking kids, alright well hopefully she stays at home now then". We swiftly move onto other topics, and he starts talking about some station gossips as my phone pings and looking down to check on it I see Grace's name, I didn't want to leave her alone tonight but we were short staffed so there was no option, and she seemed happy enough to stay by herself. When I open the message though, panic overtakes me as the blood drains from my face and my heart starts racing. Throwing my phone at Mike, I speed off to her house, hoping we get there in time. It's on the other side of town, and I panic knowing it's going to take a good 15 minutes to get there.

"What the fuck, Jaxx, where are you going?" He gives me a puzzled look as I shove the lights and siren on the car to get to her faster. "Read my phone, Grace is in trouble!" his eyes move down to my phone, and I get a side view of his eyes going wide as he reads the message". "Shit, I'll call it in for backup in case there is someone closer".

I nod to him, unable to physically form words right now, and around 10 minutes later, after possibly breaking every speed limit there is, I pull on to the top of her street speeding down it, stopping short when I see smoke coming from the front of the house. "Fuck, I'm going in" I shout to Mike and don't even wait for his response before grabbing my jacket and putting it in front of my face.

The house is filled with smoke, and I can barely see a thing, "Grace" I shout out, hoping she's still conscious, or under better circumstances not even in the house. I'm about to run up the stairs when I spot her motionless foot sticking out from between the sofas, causing me to stop short. I feel like the world stops right there as I realise she could very well be dead already, but I push it to the back of my head, running over to her and crouch down beside her still body, "Grace, Grace, Sweetheart. Talk to me". Turning her over I spot blood on her face, her cheek slightly swollen and a bruise forming under her eye. *"Fuck"* I say out loud to myself. I bring my hand to her throat as I check her pulse, it's there but it's weak, thankfully she's just passed out. The flames surrounding us flick up at me as they spread quicker by the minute, and I know I need to move fast if I want to get us both out alive.

My eyes scan the room as I try to figure out an escape so we don't get into anymore danger, and I spot the back door with less smoke surrounding it than the front of the house. Scooping her up into my arms, I cover us both with my jacket as much as I can and run for the back door. When I get to it I'm thankful to find it unlocked, although I hope that's not how he got in here. The thought leaves my head just as soon as it enters though, and I'm moving as fast as my feet will take me, calling out to Mike for help as I come around to the front of the house. When I get to there, I'm thankful to see that Mike has already called in EMT as they pull up outside just as I'm rounding the corner. Fire rescue pulls up a second later, and they jump out and into action. I make a dart for the ambulance, as the paramedic takes her from me asking for her information as he works.

"Her name is Grace Vale, 26, she's been attacked and we are on the lookout for the suspect, I'm good to assume he has left the house already, so she is the only casualty, please work fast”. He nods to me, and the other paramedic pulls me back slightly, so they can work on her. Her soot covered body looks pale and lifeless on the gurney as they place an oxygen mask over her nose and mouth.

The first paramedic looks back up to me, “Thank you, Sheriff, we will take it from here”. I stop short and scowl at him, clearly forgetting he has no clue who I am to her. “No, I'm not going anywhere, that's my girlfriend you're working on” I say, pointing to where Grace is lying. “Oh” they look at each other briefly then back to me, “Okay we need to get her to the hospital and fast, are you coming with us?” I look back to where Mike is, and he nods his head to me “Go, I'll wait for backup to arrive and sort out here, you just go be with Grace. I'll get her family's info and give them a call, so don't worry about that either”. Nodding my thanks to him, I grab the handles and haul myself into the back of the ambulance where I silently take a seat and watch them work on her more. One of the paramedics jumps out and rounds to the front of the ambulance to get us to the nearest hospital, the other working on Grace as we drive. “She's inhaled a lot of smoke, but I think she's going to be okay, you got to her just in time. We just need to keep monitoring her for a little while as it looks like she's taken a nasty bump to the head. I'll get the doctors to do a scan to make sure there’s nothing serious, but her pupils are reactive so that’s a good sign”. I numbly nod to him, unable to form words.

It feels like it takes so long to get to the hospital, but when we do they rush her in straight away, getting her hooked up to machines while I watch on from the door before I'm pushed out and into the waiting room, the nurse takes one look at me and hands me some water whilst pointing to the chairs behind me "Sit. You should get checked on too, did you go into the fire for her?" she asks looking back at the room Grace is in. I keep staring ahead at her room as I respond, "Yes I did but I'm fine, just help her please". I down my water, handing the cup back to the nurse, she doesn't look too convinced but goes along with it, "Okay but if you start to experience any symptoms, you get checked out straight away". "Yeah sure, I will." I distractedly reply, but it satisfies her enough that she nods and walks off, leaving me alone in my thoughts".

My head drops into my hands and for the first time in a long time I let myself cry; the thought I could have lost her tonight for good is too much right now to stop the tears flowing. I could still lose her, but I'm desperately trying to hold on to the fact the paramedic assured me she would be fine. I stay like that, silently crying, shoulders shaking a little as I do, but my moment is interrupted when Tristan comes barrelling into the waiting room.

"Where is she?" He snaps out, looking around as if she's going to be sitting next to me. His mom, dad and Lilly all follow behind him, solemn expressions on their faces. I let out a sigh, standing and coming face to face with Tristan, "She's being seen to, the paramedic thinks she will be okay, she just inhaled a lot of smoke" I say, trying to reassure them. "Oh thank god", his mom cries from behind him, and I turn to face her, momentarily distracted when I'm shoved by Tristan. I stumble a little looking back at him, my brows scrunched into a frown as I'm confused by his sudden change in attitude, but then he opens his mouth and I see red. "You were supposed to fucking look after her and look at this mess. Why are you even here if you can't do that one thing". "Tristan, enough" his dad barks, but I'm already too far gone to care, so I lay into him.

"I have been looking after her, she's been with me all fucking week. I'm sorry that I had to go and do my fucking job Tristan, but I didn't see you calling up to sit with her did I? He's not been spotted all week, so I didn't think he was just going to turn up and fucking try to kill her!" I raise my voice to him as I get in his face. It's unprofessional given my role but I need him to realise I'm not the one to blame for this, "I have had people looking into him and trying to sort this shit out whilst making sure she's been okay. Not once this week have you offered to help whilst she's been by herself knowing yourself that he was still out there, especially after you demanded that I keep her safe, so if you want to blame anyone, then fucking blame yourself. I'm going outside to cool off and when I come back you better have either changed your attitude or fuck off, because I'm not in the mood for your shit tonight".

I turn on my heel and storm out of the hospital waiting room, making it outside as I collapse against the wall, the cold evening doing nothing to cool the rage building inside me right now. I'm shaking I'm that angry with him, but I try to remember his position as her brother, and that he's probably just as upset as me. I shouldn't have spoken to him like that but he fucking wound me up.

Shutting my eyes, I let my head fall back against the cool brick for a moment so I can gather my thoughts, when someone coughs from beside me pulling me from my internal battle. I peek a look at who's standing with me and see Harold lighting a cigarette before offering me one. I shake my head and he shrugs his shoulders, lifting his own cigarette to his mouth and taking a long drag of it.

He stands beside me silently for a moment, so I decide to fill that silence and apologise to him for my behaviour. "Sir I just want to apologise for the way I lashed out back there, I know it's not Tristan's fault or anyone's for that matter..." He holds up his hand, cutting me off. "Jaxx don't apologise to me, my son is a stubborn asshole that doesn't know his head from his ass some days, I know you were just doing right by my Grace, and at the end of the day, it was you who pulled her out of the fire tonight. If it wasn't for you she.." he chokes up a little, clearing his throat before continuing, "Anyway I'm glad that you are here for her, but why don't you go home and get some rest and a shower, we will stay here with her and you come back once your sorted".

Shaking my head at him I swallow back the tears I feel threatening to fall, "I'm staying until she's awake. I can't leave her side until I know she's okay". He smiles back at me, his height almost matching mine. Patting me on the shoulder once, he pulls me into a hug. “I'm glad you found her son, you're good for her”.

I pull back a little from him, now seems a good time as any to mention it. “I also want to ask, I know it’s probably not the most ideal time to, but now seems a good a time as any. I'm not going to just yet, but I want to ask Grace to be my wife. I feel like I needed to ask you first. I mean I will be doing it regardless, so this is more of just a pre warning”.

He lets out a laugh at me, shaking his head as he pats my back once more, “I'm glad you told me, but you would have had my permission either way son”. He holds out his hand to me and I take it, giving him a firm handshake. “I won't let you down, I just need her to hurry and wake back up so I can finally ask her”. I chuckle a little, but my mind instantly goes back to her in that room.

Harold tips his head in the direction of the hospital, “Shall we go back inside?” I nod to him, and we make our way back into the building, stopping off to grab some coffee for everyone on the way. When we get back to the waiting area, I hand a coffee to Tristan, and he takes it from me grumbling a thank you. I know I won’t get a proper apology from him, so I just walk off shaking my head at my asshole best friend.

We aren't waiting long before the doctor comes back through with news on Grace. “She's still unconscious, but we're happy with the scans, and she's got a pretty nasty bump to her head and some concussion, as well as some bad smoke inhalation and a swollen ankle. We've checked it and it doesn't seem to be broken, so we're going to monitor her, but she should wake up soon if you would like to go in and sit with her." We all thank the doctor and head into the room to see her.

She's been cleaned up a little but not enough, and the nurse has put her into a gown. The oxygen mask is on her face still, and she looks so tiny in that bed. I go straight to her side, taking her hand as I lean in and press a kiss to her head, her dad pulls a chair for her mom to sit on the other side of her and then comes round to put one under me for me to sit down too. Lily waits on the back wall of the room with her brother, and I gesture for her to swap with me, but she smiles shaking her head at me, tears streaking her face.

I sit there in my thoughts for a moment, watching numbly as her chest moves up and down, but I can't sit there for long, so I get to my feet needing to go out of the room to cool off. I don't know if I can bare to see her looking like that much longer. Her body still and lifeless, the creamy skin on her arms and face covered in the soot from the fire.

I lean my arms onto the wall outside her room, bending slightly at the waist, and put my head between them trying to breathe through it, but a sob breaks free from my throat, and I just allow it as I cry some more. The memory of her laying in the bed and looking so innocent and helpless, now seared into my brain. I jump a little when I feel a hand come to my back, and when I look up Tristan is stood looking at me frowning down at me as he takes my form in. I scoff at him letting my head fall back between my shoulders, "If you've come to make any more shitty comments then you can take them and kindly fuck off". I see him shuffle on his feet for a second thinking he might actually walk away, but he surprises me with an apology making me eat my words "I just want to say I'm sorry, I didn't mean to take it out on you like that. I know it isn't your fault, I just... fuck, I just want her to wake up" I slowly bring myself to standing and turn to face him, watching as a small tear streaks down his cheek, and fuck if that doesn't start me off again.

"C'mere you fucking asshole". I grab the back of his head and pull him into me giving him a hug and he lets the tears flow more freely. Anyone would think Grace died the way were going at it, but we don't show this emotion to anyone often, and I'm not about to stop now. He pulls back after calming himself down, holding me at arm's length, then brings his hand out in front of me. "We good?" I look down at his outstretched hand then back up to him, a smile breaking across my face for the first time all dam day.

Taking his hand, I shake it gripping the top of his shoulder with my other, "Yeah were good. Don't fucking speak to me like that again though or I'll throw your ass in lockup, got it?" He laughs back at me clearly thinking I'm joking but I would do it just to take the piss out of him. "Got it, Sherriff". He gives me a little mock salute and then spins on his heel walking back into Grace's room. *Fucking asshole.*

After a while Grace's family all go home to get some rest, and I assure them I'll give them a call as soon as she wakes up. The doctors come in and out checking on her throughout the night, letting me know she could stay asleep for a while and so I should go home but I just can't leave her right now, so I settle into the chair next to her bed ready for a long night ahead.

31

Grace

BEEP *BEEP* *BEEP*

I wake up feeling stiff and disorientated, trying to figure out my surroundings, my head is pounding, and I try to open my eyes, but it's bright in the room so I have to squint until they adjust. "Urgh" I groan out loud, trying to will my stiff muscles to move, and peaking my eyes open fully when I see movement in the corner of my eye. Jaxx is sitting in the corner, stuffed into a hospital chair like a piece of origami in his work uniform, he looks exhausted, and I wonder how long he's been here at my bedside. He's covered in soot, and the smell of smoke drifts over to my nose causing me to have a flashback, taking me back to the last time I remember being awake.

The sardonic smile on Liam's face as I'm left lying on the living room floor to die. He looks over to the curtain as it begins to catch fire before blowing me a kiss and walking to the back door, slipping out into the cool night air, trapping me in, my legs are trying to move but my head won't allow it. I'm trapped in my own body and I'm going to die here.

I suck in a sharp breath of air as I come back to reality and sit up a little too quickly causing pain to shoot through my body and making me to cry out. The noise I make wakes Jaxx and he's up and straight out of his chair coming to my side in an instant. "Grace, shit your awake. Sweetheart lie back down, you're in the hospital, you've been out for a few hours because you were in a house fire, but you're okay now". I rapidly shake my head from side to side, tears beginning to stream down my face, "Liam, he did this" I croak out as a sob breaks free, Jaxx cradles my head comforting me, "Shh it's okay, I know he did this and we will find him, don't worry about a thing". I grip on to his shirt, my fingers digging into the fabric, as I sob harder into him, knowing this wasn't just a bad dream, and Liam actually tried to kill me.

It takes me a minute or two to calm down again, as Jaxx strokes my smoke-filled hair trying to soothe me. When he pulls back, his gaze lingers on my face, searching, before he sits on the edge of the bed beside me and hands me a glass of water. I drink it down quickly, then pass the empty glass back, which he sets on the side table. He turns to me again, gently taking my hand in his, a flicker of hesitation in his eyes. "Do you remember what happened, Grace?" he asks softly. I nod, swallowing, uncertain if I trust my voice just yet. "Do you think you can tell me what happened?" he urges, his tone calm but full of concern.

I let out a deep sigh, leaning back into the bed again, and shut my eyes as I try to collect my thoughts. I eventually reopen them, feeling the tears threatening to drop from my eyes so I blink them back a couple of times. With a croaky voice I begin "He turned up at the house. I thought it was one of the kids coming for candy, so I opened the door, and he caught me off guard. I.. I tried to escape from him but he got the bathroom door open and got to me, and I think I fell down the stairs a little and twisted my ankle so he caught up with me, he um.. He hit me a couple of times and then pushed me down, and I think I must have hit my head on the coffee table. I saw him moving the candles near to the curtain to start the fire, but I couldn't move, and I passed out after that".

He looks at me, his face softening with pity, and I quickly look away, unable to meet his gaze. "Don't look at me like that Jaxx, I don't need you to feel sorry for me, it's my own fault. I should have been more careful, and I wasn't". He squeezes my hand a little, bringing his other one to my chin as he lifts my face to meet his, "I don't pity you Grace, you are the bravest person I know, you just survived a house fire, and I am just so grateful that you're still here right now".

Tears fall freely now, and I pull him into me clutching on to him like my life depends on it. He holds me for a minute longer before letting me go, we sit there silently for a moment when I remember what happened to the house, "Oh god the house. What's happened to the house? Is it destroyed?!" I feel panic creeping back up my throat, because it's not just my home, it's Rose and Hallie's too. His eyes shift to the side slightly, like he's about to lie, but he thinks better of it. His eyes drop down as he lets out a sigh, before he brings them back up to meet mine as he tells me "The house needs quite a bit of repairs, but the insurance will cover it. I've spoken to the girls, and they know, they are waiting until we get you home to come and see you". I can't help myself and start crying again "I don't have a home anymore Jaxx, where the hell am I going to live".

His hand comes up to wipe the tears from my cheeks as he waits for me to calm down a little before speaking, "You can move in with me for the time being, I'm not letting you out of my sight at least until Liam is found and if you still want to find your own place once we have him then we can look for somewhere for you, but if you will consider it then I'd like you to move in with me permanently". My eyes flick to his, a frown taking over my face. "You want me to move in with you?" My brain isn't working properly clearly, because he lets out a small chuckle nodding to me. "Yes Grace, I want you to move in with me, I want to wake up with you every day, and go to sleep with you every night. I've loved being with you this past week, and I don't want that to stop anytime soon, so will you please consider it?"

I look at him, slightly perplexed by the whole situation, but I don't think I could go back to not being with him every day either, so I nod to him, a small smile touching my lips. "I think that I want to live with you too Jaxx". His eyes go wide, and his cheeks break out into the biggest grin. "Thank fuck for that, because

I actually wasn't going to let you leave me anyway". I giggle at his comment as he leans into me, pressing his lips to mine in a gentle kiss, I feel myself wanting to get carried away in the moment, so I press myself a little more into him, letting out a soft moan and allowing him more access. His tongue sweeps my bottom lip caressing them, before deepening the kiss, but were interrupted by someone stood in the doorway, coughing a little to let us know they are there. We both stop, and I peak over his shoulder to see the nurse coming in with a knowing smile on her face.

"Oh good you're awake. I'll get the doctor to come and check over you, but if you're feeling up to it and the doctor gives you the all clear, you should be able to go home soon if you like". I smile and nod back to her, "God yes, no offence but I hate hospitals", I let out an exaggerated shiver, causing the nurse to laugh at me before she goes to get the doctor.

Jaxx leaves the room to get us both a coffee and a short while later, Dr. Johnson who's been looking at my scans and monitoring me, comes in to check me over, once he's satisfied with all my answers and checks he looks at my chart again before looking back up to me, "Looks like you're good to go. Just get yourself plenty of fresh air to keep your lungs healthy and we will arrange any pain meds for you, and you can be on your way", I muster up my best smile for him, hoping it will convince him enough that I'm definitely okay to leave soon, "Sure thing doc, thanks so much for all your help", as he's leaving, Jaxx comes back into the room with his brow raised, waiting for me to tell him what the doctor said, I reach out for the coffee in his hand as he passes a cup to me, taking a long sip before telling him what the doctor said.

"The doctor said I can go home once I have a prescription filled, so can you help me get dressed please". I give him my biggest grin and he returns a cheeky one of his own. Coming closer to the bed he leans down onto it, brushing his lips against mine "I most certainly can help with that, I can't promise to be a gentleman about it though" he leans back a bit and gives me a pantie dropping wink, causing heat to flood my core and oh god, I can't wait to get home and back in bed with this man.

Home. With Jaxx, the thought brings a different kind of warmth to my heart, and I sink back into the bed a little, the thought of us about to go back and live together for real this time filling me with a new kind of excitement.

32

Jaxx

“Will you stop fussing, I'm fine”.

Grace slaps my hand away for the hundredth time since we left the hospital. My hands find my hips and I tip my head back letting out a low groan, “Grace for fucks sake, will you stop trying to do everything yourself and just let me carry you into the goddam house, look” I say pointing to her shoeless feet, “You can't even walk properly on your ankle because of the sprain, so let me just get you to the bed, please”.

She scowls at me from the passenger seat of my car, hands folded over her chest while her legs dangle out of the side door. She's wearing a little pink tracksuit that I managed to hunt down in the hospital gift shop, when we realised she had no clothes with us as her pyjamas were ruined, and she didn't want to wait for me to call someone to bring something for her, this became the next best option. Her pouty bottom lip pokes out, making her seem childlike right now, maybe more so because she's acting like a child and won’t let me help. “I'm perfectly capable of getting myself into the house Jaxx, just let me do it myself”. I huff out a breath, take a step to the side, and hold my hand out towards the front door, “Go for it then, show me how capable you are”.

She sticks her chin up at me defiantly as she climbs to her feet, and I have to ball my hands into fists to stop myself from helping her right now, because she's trying to act like she doesn't need it. I’m just waiting for her to realise she needs to get from the car into the house unaided, because there’s nothing close for her to grip onto but me. She hops on one foot a few times, trying to get balance, and attempts to hop her way into the house, like she's some sort of fucking rabbit.

Before she even makes it two jumps though, she stumbles slightly and grips onto the car door for dear life. Her wide eyes shoot up to me and I roll mine back at her, a smirk tipping up on my lips. Bending down quickly I scoop her up into my arms and she lets out a little squeal, wrapping her arms around my neck. I turn to face her, my lips so close I can feel her breath on them and growl a little when I speak “Stop being a little brat and let me help you, it makes both our lives easier”. I press a quick kiss to her lips, and she huffs out a sigh at me, but quickly snuggles into my neck making me laugh at her up and down emotions today.

By the time we made it out of the hospital, the sun was coming up in the sky, signalling the start of the new day. I called into work to let them know I'd be taking a few personal days to get Grace back on the mend and sort a few bits out at home. They had someone on standby covering me quickly, and now all I need is my bed. I walk us through my house and to the downstairs guest room where I deposit a confused looking Grace on the bed.

She scrunches her face up looking around the room, and I take a step back watching her reaction, whilst raising my brow and crossing my arms. She spots the motion, looking up at me. "Why have you brought us in here?" I let out a laugh bending down to her level, "Guest room not up to your standards?" She looks confused for a second, before quickly shaking her head, "No I mean why are we in here and not your room, do you not want to share a bed with me?" her bottom lip comes out into a pout and she looks up to me, her bright green eyes shining in the morning light.

"Sweetheart, first of all it's our bedroom now not mine, and second, you can't get from the car to the house by yourself, so how did you think you were going to get down the stairs without needing me too? I'm sleeping in here too, it's just easier for the next few days until you can put weight on your ankle again, that's all". She lets out a breath looking up to me, her pout changing to a cheesy little smile, and her green eyes sparkle with mischief "Oh good, I thought you were going to leave me all alone".

I toe my shoes off and crawl onto the bed to hover over her, my knees either side of her legs, as I work to keep my arms straight, stopping me from falling onto her "Now why would I do that baby girl, you know full well you aren't leaving my sight for the next week at least". Her fingers come up to play with my shirt which is still covered in soot, I really should go and get a shower, but I need to be with her for just a minute longer. I press a soft kiss to her lips, and she moans into it, the little sounds coming from her instantly making me hard. “Baby, don't make noises like that, I really need to get cleaned up, and I need to help you get a shower too”.

She wiggles her brows at me, her hips doing a little shimmy of their own too, and I know instantly what she’s thinking. “How about you run us a bath then and we can get cleaned up together, saves me trying to stand for too long”, I close my eyes hanging my head slightly, and giving it a little shake whilst laughing at her attempt to seduce me, “I take it you’re feeling a little better already”, she nods her head quickly to me, and I laugh a little more at the excited expression on her face. “If it wasn't for this stupid ankle, I'd say I'm just fine Jaxx” she releases her hold on my shirt lifting her arms and wiggling her fingers at me, “C'mon, I’ll let you help me this time, get me soaped up baby”.

I bark out a laugh, and she giggles back at me. Standing from the bed, I look down at her for a minute before doing just as she asks and scoop her up, taking us both into the bathroom where I prop her on the vanity whilst I fill the tub. Whilst it’s filling, I turn and strip us both off starting with her first whilst waiting for it to finish, and once it is I lift her again turning to lower her in, she hisses a little at the heat, and as I look down I notice the bruising on her stomach. My hands go straight to it, dusting over the deep purple marks marring her perfect creamy flesh, I feel myself getting annoyed that I didn't even spot it when we were in the hospital. “Are you sure you're okay Grace, those bruises look really nasty” I trace them with my fingertips, wishing I could have been there with her. She looks down at them, shrugs and looks back up to me seemingly unaffected by all the bruising on her face and body, “Yeah I’ll be fine, they aren't actually that bad. I'm a tough cookie you know”, she says winking at me. I’m a little more wary now than I was before, but she notices straight away from the look on my face, “Jaxx I’m fine, get in the tub before I wash myself”. I shoot her an eye roll “Alright bossy, scoot up so I can get in behind you”. She does as I ask, causing the water to slosh around in the tub a little as I climb in behind her.

I pull her back to rest against me, grabbing the sponge off the side and lathering it up with soap. I try to be gentle around her bruising as I clean her all over whilst washing myself at the same time, then I get her to sit up so I can wash her hair for her. I lather up the shampoo in my hands and begin massaging her scalp with my fingers and she lets out a little moan at the action. “Keep that up baby and your hair won’t be the only thing I'm massaging” I say to her, and she lets out a little chuckle.

“Maybe I want you to massage somewhere else Jaxx”. Her comment comes out breathily like she can't quite get her words out, and because I don't want to ruin the moment, I quickly rinse the shampoo from her hair and pull her back towards me. My dick hardens almost painfully under her ass cheeks as I bring my hand up, cupping my fingers around her neck, flexing them gently so that I don’t hurt her. She feels my dick pressing against her and wiggles her hips into me a little more. Bringing my other hand up to her hair, I tug at it a little, pulling her back into me, so my lips are next to her cheek. "Stop moving baby, or I won't be able to contain myself and this will be a very disappointing bath for you".

She giggles again but stops moving, and I let my hand smooth down her smooth wet skin, over the peaks of her breasts, stopping and giving one a massage, I pinch at her nipple rolling it between my fingers until it forms in to a hard peak, once I'm satisfied with that one my fingers skim over her skin to her other breast doing the same motion, while my other hand still cups her neck, squeezing it ever so slightly. She lets out a little moan, giving me the confirmation I want to go ahead and continue my journey down to her perfect little pussy. My fingers trace over her hip bone and her legs part just enough for me to be able to slip my hand between them and to the silky smooth skin there.

I stroke over her slit a couple of times before dipping my finger inside and pressing gently on her clit. She hisses out a breath as I work my fingers up and down the sensitive little bundle of nerves there, moving a little to push a finger inside her, I pump in and out a few times coating myself with her wetness, then bringing it back up to rub against her clit again. She moans louder into my ear, so I bring my hand up to cup her jaw, tipping her head slightly towards me and pressing a kiss to it. I continue the motion as my fingers work in and out of her, adding a second one and bringing my thumb up to her clit to bring her to the edge quicker. I press my lips to her ear, my gravelly voice murmuring into it "I need to be inside you baby, but you're gonna come for me here first, and then I'll give you another when we get back to bed, think you can manage that?" She moans into me "Yess, ahh Jaxx yes, yes".

I chuckle into her ear, stroking her more "That's a good girl, now give me what I want from you baby". I push my fingers in and out of her a few more times, bringing my other hand down to rub her clit harder whilst my fingers move inside her, and I feel her walls start to contract around my fingers, she moans loudly letting her head fall back against my chest, and I press feather light kisses to the top of her shoulder, "That's it baby, come for me". Her walls clench around my fingers hard as her release takes a hold of her, and I continue my motions as she comes down from the orgasm that's taken over her body.

I give her a minute to come back to me, kissing her all over so she doesn't lose the high she's riding right now. Pulling myself out of the tub, I reach and grab a towel, drying myself as quick as I can before helping her out and wrapping her in a towel too. My arms come down, drying her over, then I pull the towel away from her, leaving her standing in front of me naked, a slight shimmer to her skin from the moisture that still lays there, small drops of water dripping down from her hair onto her bare breasts.

My hands skim over her body, wrapping around her waist as I pull her into me slightly, her hands come up to wrap around my neck as I lean down, bringing one nipple into my mouth and playing with it on my tongue, before moving on to the other to give that same attention there. Her moan floats into my ears like silk, and my dick becomes painfully hard again. I press it into her between her legs, giving myself a little bit of friction to keep me going until I get her to bed. Bringing arms down to where her legs begin, I wrap my hands around them, and in one swift motion I pull her up and over my shoulder, causing her to let out a little scream. “Jaxx, put me down” she cries out as I smack her ass, which works at shutting her up and begin marching back out the bathroom as I start towards the stairs, but I think better of it and throw her onto the bed in *our room.* I can always take her back downstairs later. She scoots up towards the headboard quickly, and I follow her up the end of it like an animal hunting its prey.

I come to rest between her legs, leaning on my forearms and into her, kissing her fiercely whilst feeling her move beneath me as her delicate body reacts to me more. I can't get enough of her right now and I don't think I ever will at this point. I'm a gone man for this woman and I will do everything I can to protect her from now on.

Her perky breasts brush up against me, the sensitive flesh hardening into little pebbles under me as I kiss down her jaw and neck, sucking on the skin in the crease of her shoulder. It tickles her a little as she lets out giggle, but it is quickly overtaken by a moan when I press my dick into her folds, moving it and causing friction, whilst move myself along her silky wetness. I pull back a little to get a look at her and her beautiful green eyes look back up to me, full of questions, “I want to make sure you're okay before I carry on, I don't want to hurt you, so I need you to tell me now if you’re hurting anywhere”.

She shakes her head smiling at me, her hand moving to grab my dick as she lines me up against her. “Put it in Jaxx and stop fucking around”. My lips tip into a smile and I nod to her, “Yes Ma’am”. I start off gentle with her, moving little by little, until she clearly gets annoyed with the pace and bucks her hips up into me. “Jaxx seriously, do the job or I’ll do it myself”. Her brow lifts as she gives me her best unimpressed look. I don't speak anymore and ram into her just like she wants, causing her to cry out a moan as she rocks her hips into me, to bring us into a synced motion.

We move together, as I work my hips into her to bring us both towards our climax, but I know she can't get there just from me fucking her, so I bring my hand down to rub her clit some more, massaging in circles as I press as deep as I can into her. It doesn't take long from that point until she's shaking under me, crying out my name whilst I come to my own release, spilling myself inside her.

I collapse on top of her, keeping as much weight as I can on my arms, so I don't hurt her. We're both a sweaty mess, panting into each other to try and catch our breath again. I stay like that for as long as I can, drinking her in, this gorgeous woman that's mine. Pressing a soft kiss to her lips, she lazily smiles up at me, heavy lidded eyes, blinking back at me as she struggles to keep them open, like she could fall asleep any second.

“I love you Grace, so fucking much. I was so scared I was going to lose you last night and I don't think I would have coped if you were more injured, hell I barely managed to keep it together as it was”. Her hand comes up to stroke my cheek and I lean into her warmth. Green eyes sparkling in the morning sunlight that's filtering through the window. Her voice is barely a whisper as she replies to me, "I love you too Jaxx, and you aren't going to lose me because I'm not going anywhere. You're stuck with me whether you like it or not". Her smile turns into a cheeky little grin, and I lean down nudging my nose against hers.

"I wouldn't want it any other way baby".

33

Jaxx

I stir to the sound of vibrating coming from somewhere in the room. It's incessant and as much as I try to ignore it, the irritating noise keeps on coming back. I try to open my eyes a few times, having to blink to adjust them, the sun is still shining through the window and so I'm not too sure on how much I've slept, but when I look to my side, Grace is still sleeping peacefully snuggled up in the duvet facing me, the bruise on her face shining against her pale complexion.

I let out a sigh, turning and climbing out of bed as carefully as I can so I don't wake her, she stirs a little but quickly nuzzles back into the bed like it's her favourite place in the world. I can't help myself, so I kneel back on the bed, brushing a few loose strands of hair off her face, and lightly press my lips to her temple, trying not to wake her still, but the need to touch her constantly has overtaken everything else since I found her in that house.

The buzzing starts again, and I have to suppress a groan, letting out a deep breath I quickly grab some sweats to pull on and go in search of my phone, finding it under a pile of our clothes on the floor. I've got missed calls from Mike at the station, Harris and my mom, and a quick glance at the time tells me we've been asleep for about 4 hours as its only 2pm, and so I go to ring Mike back but it begins ringing in my hand again, I quickly answer it putting the phone to my ear as I leave the room, I pull the door shut and then respond, “Hey Harris, sorry Grace is sleeping and I didn't want to disturb her, what’s up?”

“I got more info back on Liam, I tried calling the station and got Mike, but he said you were off with Grace after a fire? Is she alright?” Ah shit I haven't even gotten around to calling him, I sigh into the phone scrubbing my hand over my face as I make my way down to the living room to take a seat, “Yeah she's fine, Liam turned up at the house and attacked her, then tried to set the house on fire with her still inside”. He lets out a low whistle on the other end of the phone, “Shit man, do you have him in custody already then? A warrant popped up on the system for his arrest, but that was a few days ago, which is actually why I'm calling you”, my interest piques and I urge him to continue. “Well, it turns out he's been hacking a few systems, including the bank. He's been following Grace online and in person since she left Atlanta by the looks of it. He’s not done a great job of hiding his tracks, hence the warrant, but I've tried to track his whereabouts over the last few days as he took out a large sum of cash and hasn't used any of his banks or phone since”.

“Mmm”, I grunt into the phone “Yeah, I can't imagine he got too far from here, but Mike has a warrant out for his arrest in a couple of counties so hopefully he's still in the state. If I find out anything before you do, then I'll let you know and same goes for you”.

"Yeah sure, thing. I'll let you get going and catch up with you soon". He replies into the phone, I mumble a goodbye back to him and end the call, dropping my phone onto the sofa next to me.

I'm sat in my thoughts for a couple of minutes, when I hear a thud come from upstairs and then Grace's groggy voice, "Owhhh fuck! That hurt". I'm up in an instant rushing to the bedroom, to find Grace's head peeking up from the other side of the bed, her body twisted up in the duvet. I come round to her side of the bed, hands on my hips trying my hardest to hold back a laugh, but she's sitting wrapped up in the duvet like it's a cocoon, her hair is wild and sticking out all over the place. "What are you doing?" I ask, she scowls up at me and huffs out a little breath, before blowing upwards to try and move her hair off her face.

"I was trying to get up, but I got twisted in the sheets and tumbled out of bed, and now I'm a little stuck, can you help me, or are you just gonna stand there laughing at me". I shake my head at her, letting out a little chuckle, to which her frown deepens a little more, "I didn't mean actually laugh at me you know". I crouch down to her level and scoop her up, depositing her back on the bed, and unravelling her from the mess she's got herself in. "I couldn't help myself, Jesus Grace how much do you move around in your sleep to get this tangled?" Her still sleepy face grins back up to me, shrugging her shoulders a little as I untangle her legs.

Once I finally get her straight again, she scoots herself to sitting further up the bed, flinching a little as she does and my eyes dart down to her stomach again.

“Are you sore?” I say coming to sit on the bed beside her, she nods slightly back at me “Hmm, a little. I think I banged my ribs a bit where I’m bruised, but I'm fine I promise”. I’m not convinced at all, so I stand from the bed and head downstairs into the kitchen to grab her some of her medication. By the time I’ve got the glass and some water for her and return to the bedroom, she's pulled a sheet around herself and is searching around for something, “Sit down and take these, I told you not to move around on your foot. And what are you even looking for?”

She huffs at me, but sits on the bed, taking the tablets from me and drinking them down with her water. She places the glass on the side table and looks back over to me, frowning slightly “I can't find my phone, did I leave it downstairs?” I had put it in on the kitchen counter as I came into the house, but it was still switched off, and it’s a good thing really because she's going to need a new one now, I know Liam was probably hacking into her phone this whole time. “It’s in the kitchen but I'll need to nip into town and get you a new one. My detective friend, Harris called before you woke up and informed me that Liam was hacking into a few different things, and we think he could have been tracking your phone this whole time. I don't want to take any chances, so I think it's probably best if you change your number too”.

I get up and begin searching around the drawers for a spare t-shirt for her as I talk to her, finding one I turn to stand and catch her wiping her eyes. “Grace what's wrong sweetheart, why are you crying?” I ask, coming back around to her side of the bed, T-shirt in hand. She looks back up to me, eyes filled with more unshed tears and shakes her head a little. "Maybe I should go stay at my parent's place for a little while. I don't want to be bringing danger to your door, if he is still keeping tabs on me, he'll know I'm here already and I don't want you getting caught up in my mess".

I feel anger go through me, but not at Grace, I feel it towards the asshole that's made her feel like she's no longer safe. She's close enough to me that I can touch her, and right now I need that so I reach out to her, my hands cupping either side of her face, "Baby you're safe here, I can protect you and I'm not going to leave you alone, so you don't have to worry about anything. I've had one of the patrol cars staying near my house on the lookout for him in case he does return, but if you ask me, he'd be very stupid to at this point. There are multiple warrants out for his arrest, and I've been told that he's taken out a large sum of cash from his bank, so it's pretty safe to assume he's gone on the run.

Her face has a dejected look on it, as the tears begin to fall. I swipe my thumb across her cheek wiping them away, and her head tips slightly as she leans into me. Her eyes flutter shut, and as she lets out a little sigh her body slumps the tiniest bit, but I notice it, "You need more rest Grace, why don't you try and go back to sleep for a little while. I'll call your sister and get her to grab some clothes for you until we can get you some more. I don't know what of yours was okay in the fire, but it took over most of the house by the time they put it out, so if you like, in a couple of days when you're feeling better, we'll go do some damage to my credit card and get you a new wardrobe, how does that sound?"

Her lips tip up into a small smile, "Are you trying to make me feel better Jaxx? cause it's definitely working". Leaning into her, I press a kiss to her soft lips, "For you sweetheart I'd do anything". "I love you Jaxx" she breathes out the words, like they're part of her. "I love you too Grace. Okay c'mon, pop this t-shirt on so you have something to wear if you need to get up and then get some more sleep and I'll make us some food and call your sister".

Grace nods, lying back down, and I tuck her back into the duvet. Standing up I lean down and stroke over her hair one last time, "I'll be back up in a little bit baby". Pressing a kiss to her temple, her eyes flutter shut, and she nods sleepily at me.

I head back downstairs and call up her sister, who answers on the 3rd ring. "Hey, is everything okay with Grace?", I look back towards the stairs briefly before replying, "Yeah, she's sleeping now, but I'm not sure she's going to have any clothes left from the fire. Do you have anything at all that she could use until we can go and get her some new bits?" She's quiet for a minute before responding to me, "Yeah, she left some clothes here last time, so I'll grab them and we're a similar size so I'll bring some of my bits that might fit her too". I nod into the phone before remembering she can't actually see me, "Thanks Lily that would be great, I need to nip out quickly, but I have someone watching the house, so I'll call by and grab them from you in the next half an hour if that's okay?" After agreeing to the time, we end the call and I quickly write a note for

Grace, slipping back into the bedroom and leaving it on the bedside table for her that I'll be back soon and to not get out of bed.

I grab some clothes from my wardrobe on the way out, take a quick shower and head out the door to grab some food and get her a new phone. I just hope I get back to the house in time before she's awake.

34

Grace

Pain runs through my body jolting me awake, and I move at such a fast pace that my whole-body hurts, causing me to cry out. I feel myself hyperventilating, my breath coming in rapidly and I can't seem to slow my heart rate, I feel like I'm having another panic attack. Pressing my hand to my chest, my skin feels cold and clammy, but my body is on fire. I feel like I'm on fire.

The nightmare which woke me, takes me straight back to the other night, and I'm overcome by a feeling of powerlessness, my body refusing to move. I crane my neck slightly hoping that Jaxx might be in the room, but it's empty, the late afternoon sun shining through the window, and the trees are blowing in the distance from the November chill. I concentrate on the beauty outside, trying to throw the hellish thoughts out of my mind, and finally after what feels like forever, I'm able to move.

Sitting myself up a little, I swing my legs around so I can get a better look out of the window and take in the view, enjoying how much it lifts my mood. I'm interrupted from my little reprieve by Jaxx coming back in, "Hey, are you okay I heard a… Grace Vale, you had better not be trying to get out of bed by yourself, I told you not to walk on your foot". He huffs out, stomping over to my side of the bed and coming to stop in front of me. My eyes flit up to watch him, and I have to say I'm secretly enjoying his little tantrum, all because he thought I was going to get up. His hands are resting low on his hips, and he's got a cute little scowl across his face, while his steely grey eyes narrow in on me by the second, and I can't help it when my lips tip up into a little smirk.

I sit back a little, resting my weight on my hands, my feet dangling over the bed as I cock my head to the side a little, my eyes focusing on him as I soak in his features. "Actually, I was waiting for you, I'm quite enjoying the princess treatment I'm getting today, so I'd like you to keep it up please". I lift my hands and clap them once showing my enthusiasm to my new role, my smirk now turning into a full-blown grin.

"Brat" he murmurs, shaking his head at me, his lips curving into a little smile, and I know I've got him in a good mood, so I carry on. Holding my arms out to him like I'm a small child I wiggle my fingers up at him a little, "I'm hungry baby, can you take me to get some food?" and batting my lashes I add on "Please".

He chuckles at me a little and comes to stand between my legs, resting his hands on the bed either side of me as he leans in close. "It's a good job I was already coming to get you, or I'd have left you up here with that attitude". He pecks me on the lips and slides his hands under my ass, "Put your arms around my neck baby" I do as he says, and he sweeps me up, pulling my legs around him as he does.

Smirking at me now, our bodies are so close I momentarily forget what he actually came to get me for "Is that better princess?" I bob my head up and down giving him my best shit eating grin, and he pecks me quickly on the lips laughing at my eagerness "Good, let's get you fed then" he says turning to walk us down the stairs, we get to the top of them though and he realises he can't quite get down them with my in the position I'm in. I expect him to put me down, but he pulls my legs from around him quickly and puts me over his shoulder. I let out a little squeal at his antics, but he carries on down the stairs so casually like I'm not literally hanging from his shoulder.

He pulls me back over his shoulder when we come into the kitchen and sits me on the stool at the island. It takes me a minute to get my bearings but once I do, I take in the view in front of me. My favourite sunflowers are sitting atop of the marble kitchen counters and he's got grilled cheese sandwiches ready and waiting. My stomach grumbles just looking at them, making my face heat with embarrassment, Jaxx chuckles at the noise and pushes the plate towards me, "Sounds like the princess is famished, eat up."

I give him a snarky look in return as he takes his seat next to me and pulls up his own plate, but I don't wait for a moment more, turning back to my own plate and devouring the greasy snack. It feels like forever since I actually ate something, but I fill up quickly, drinking the lemonade he's poured for the two of us as I go. I eat in what must be record timing, as I sit back in my chair tapping my stomach. "That was the best grilled cheese I've had in ages, who would have thought such a simple meal could be so good". Jaxx smiles over to me, popping the last bite of his sandwich into his mouth, and chewing thoughtfully before answering. "You know, if I had known you would be such an easy person to please, I wouldn't have tried so hard with the fancy restaurant, I'd have just brought you here and made you grilled cheese sandwiches for dinner.

I laugh back at his comment, tapping my finger against my lips, "Yeah you could have, but now you've earned yourself extra brownie points for the flowers and sandwich, so I think you could take that as a win". He grins at me shaking his head a little as he gets up to collect the plates and takes them over to the sink, once he's put them in, he turns and bends down to grab a bag from the floor. "I picked up some clothes from Lily's and nipped into town to get you a phone whilst you were sleeping, so we can set that up this afternoon if you like. I can get everyone's numbers you need copied over for you", I look up at him, smiling, overwhelmed by the thoughtfulness in every little detail. He's literally taken care of everything, anticipating even the smallest things I'd need—and still, he thought to get me flowers. It's such a simple gesture, yet it fills me with a warmth I can't put into words.

....

After having lunch and setting up my new phone, I messaged Hallie and Rose to let them know I was back home, and they let me know they are both on

Office for National Statistics

their way back in to town to see me and start making arrangements to sort the house, I feel absolutely awful that their home is ruined too, so I checked with Jaxx and then asked them to come over for the evening if they were free, and now its 7pm and I'm waiting impatiently for my best friends to arrive.

The doorbell goes and Jaxx gets up to answer it, letting Hallie and Rose in and they come rushing to where I'm sitting in the living room. He goes to the kitchen to make them both drinks as they take up space next to me on the sofa. I told Jaxx he didn't need to stay in if he wanted to go out, but he quickly informed me that my brother and Luca were coming round too, so it was going to be a nice evening with our friends, good food and plenty of wine.

He comes back quickly with their drinks, handing us some takeaway menus when the door goes again, and he goes to get it. Rose's head snaps toward the direction of the door, "Who else is coming round?" But before I get a chance to answer Luca speaks up from behind Rose "Well, no one told me you were coming Red". Rose rolls her eyes at him whilst still facing me and I have to bite my lip to hold back the laugh that wants to burst out of me. She turns to face him then tipping her head to the side, "What kind of a name is red?"

My head swivels between her and Luca watching the exchange, Luca's face breaks out into a grin as he plops himself down on the opposite sofa, "You have red hair, and well I like it so that's what I'm calling you". He props his ankle up over his opposite knee and stretches his hands behind his head like they're having the most casual conversation, but I see the irritability in Rose's face. She points a finger at him, "Don't be so fucking childish Luca, and my name is Rose so use it, I didn't give you permission to call me any nicknames". He just smiles back at her, "Nah I'm good *Red.*"

I slide my gaze over to the others to see if any of them are catching onto this little exchange, but the only person that seems to be paying any attention like I am, is Jaxx. He has a small smile playing on his lips like he knows something no one else does. Hallie and Tristan are discussing plans for the house, and so I tune my ears to that conversation instead to join in. "Where are you going to stay Hallie?" My brother asks from his spot on the floor. The house isn't massive so there are only two sofas and Tristan has decided to lounge on the rug in front of the fire, whilst Jaxx has sat next to Luca on the other sofa. He's got his legs crossed over each other and is stretched out on the floor, leaning on his elbow whilst talking to Hallie. "Oh, I'm staying with my brother until the house is finished, so I'll be out of town for a little while. To be honest, I'm not enjoying working for my dad anymore and my brother could use the help, so I've been enrolled as the temp nanny for Oliver until he sorts something more permanent, and I don't mind, it's what I'm trained for after all so this job will do me a favour".

"How long has the insurance said the house will take?" I ask, trying to get caught up on what's going on. She looks in thought for a moment before answering "They have said around six months, the extent of the damage was worse than it looks so it might just take some time". I instantly feel bad for causing so many problems for them "Oh god Hallie, I'm so sorry for all of this I feel awful. Please tell me what I can do to help". She turns to me giving me a pointed look, and I'm scared for a minute that she could actually fall out with me over this, but I really should know better by now with her. "Grace don't be ridiculous; all I want you to concentrate on is getting yourself fully healed and back to normal. We have sorted everything, so you don't need to worry". Reaching over to me she pats me on the leg reassuringly and it eases the worry I have over the situation. Turning to Rose, I ask her where she is staying too, she looks down briefly and I instantly know she's going to be staying in the last place on earth she wants to be. "I'm going to have to go to my dad's when this job finishes. I really don't want to, but I don't have any other choice".

"Wait I'm confused" my brother interjects "Why don't you want to stay at your dad's I thought you and him got on really well". She blows out a long breath before replying, "Yeah, I love my dad so much and we get on amazing, I just can't stand my mom. I don't even know why he's stayed with her for so long. She's literally so evil but he won't divorce her, says he's fine as he is, and so I only see him if we go for dinner or he comes to my place, but I have no other options so..." She shrugs her shoulders as she says it, and I feel awful that she's stuck in this situation because of me. I'm in my head for a minute trying to figure out somewhere else for her to stay when Luca speaks, "Stay at mine".

All our heads snap to Luca, he's sitting so casually like he didn't just offer up his place to an almost stranger. Rose lets out a little laugh and shakes her head at him, “Luca you barely know me, and I barely know you. I think you might regret asking me that tomorrow”. He shakes his head back at her, “Rose, you need a place, and I have a spare room. You still have another few weeks left on the job you're doing, so just think about it. If you decide you really don't want to after a couple of weeks at my place, then I'm sure we can find something else for you after that. But if you and your mom really don't get on then what's the harm in staying with me? I'm hardly ever there any way, as I stay in the city a lot, so it will be like you have your own place”.

Jaxx shoots Luca a look, scoffing a little which causes Luca’s eyes to shift to his friend but they quickly come back to Rose, I can see the cogs turning in Rose's head, mulling it over. “Look, take my number and have a think about it, you said you have a few weeks left on the job don't you, so just let me know in a couple of weeks, just trying to help you out, and if you're a friend of Grace's then you're a friend of mine”. Jaxx shakes his head again at Luca and gets to his feet looking annoyed, but Luca keeps his focus on Rose. “Yeah okay, I'll think about it”. I don't think I've ever seen Luca look so pleased with himself. He's the biggest player I think I've ever met, so if he thinks he has a chance with Rose, then he's going to be in for a surprise, but I keep my opinions to myself whilst watching the exchange between the two of them.

“So, Grace, when are you going to start working with me at the ranch?” My brother asks, bringing my attention back to him. Crap I completely forgot I said I'd do that. “Uhh, I need to sort out with Rose's dad when to finish, to be honest it's completely slipped my mind and I've not even told him I'm leaving, so I need to do that before anything”. Tristan nods in understanding, “Alright no rush, mom and dad aren't planning on going until the new year anyway, so it's enough time for us to get sorted out with everything”.

The conversation moves on to easier topics after that, and we order Chinese food in, enjoying the rest of the evening together. I spot Rose looking over in Luca's direction throughout the night and begin to wonder if maybe I'm getting the wrong end of it by assuming Rose isn't interested. Either way it's nice to all be able to hang out together, putting the last couple of weeks behind us.

35

Jaxx

A week after Grace got back from the hospital, and after waiting what feels like forever, my phone rings with a call from Harris. He has been trying to find Liam for me, as well as everyone else at the station, whilst I've been home with Grace as much as I can. It’s not helped my stress levels in the slightest, and I think my bad mood has rubbed off on her a little. She's been having nightmares, and so neither of us are getting much sleep, but thankfully she's back walking on her ankle and has used that as an excuse to go to work and speak to her boss about leaving the company.

I feel awful the amount I’ve been snapping at her the past few days, and I just hope she doesn't regret moving in with me. But I offered to drive her and wait today as she still doesn't have her car, so I'm currently sitting doing work on my laptop from the parking lot across from her work, and now hopefully getting some information from Harris. Seeing his number I answer instantly, “Hey, have you got some info for me?” He’s quick to reply, so I'm not on pins. “Hey, Jaxx. Yeah, I have good news. Liam has been spotted coming out of a motel about an hour away from where you are. I thought he would have gone further, but maybe he was keeping tabs on what's happened with Grace".

My blood runs cold at the thought of him still lurking around, and now I'm really glad that I offered to bring her to work. The last thing I want right now is to leave her exposed to him. I sigh down the phone with relief, "That's great news, can you send me everything you've got, and I'll have it sent over to the next county to get his arrest sorted". He chuckles into the phone, "Jaxx, I've already made the calls before ringing you. He should be getting picked up anytime soon. I called in a few favours and a friend at the local PD there is getting the arrest set up now".

My head falls back against the seat as I blow out a long breathe. Thank fuck he has been spotted so soon, hopefully this won't take too long now. "That's great, thank you so much for all your help. I'll let Grace know and update the station, I owe you one for this". "I'll cash in on that one-day Jaxx, but for now I'm just glad that I could help you out. I'll let you know when they have made an arrest".

We hang up and I feel my mood lifting, better than it has been for days and I shoot over a message to Mike letting him know and to tell the other guys working on the case. A couple of minutes later, Grace comes back to the car, still not looking in the best of moods but hopefully I can cheer her up with this. Climbing back in the car, she turns to look at me letting out a breath before telling me about her meeting, "He wasn't super happy with me leaving, but has said I can go whenever I feel I want to. I explained that it was the family business I'm going to, and he said he understands, I just feel so bad that I've taken a job and now I'm leaving after only a few weeks".

I pull her into me as I try to console her a little. She needs to not be worrying about work when she still needs time to properly get back to some sort of normal. "Don't worry too much about it. You're still off for the next week anyway, Rose called her dad when you went to hospital, so he knows the score". "I know, and he's said he's not upset with me, he's just gutted that he's losing me so soon, but I can't help feeling guilty, you know?" pressing a kiss to her head I hug her a little closer to me, "Yeah, I know baby girl. But don't worry about it, if he says he's fine with it then try not to worry too much. You're doing the right thing by going to work at the ranch with Tristan. And anyway, I have some news that might make you feel a little better".

She pulls back a little, looking up to me from her side of the car, and I continue "Harris called whilst you were inside, and he's said they think they have found Liam. He's hopefully getting arrested today". Her eyes close and she takes a deep breath before opening them again and looking up to me, sparkly green iris's shining with unshed tears, "Thank god for that, I can't wait for this to all just be over, it's too much to deal with, and the nightmares. I don't know if they will ever go away". She looks so down right now, that my heart breaks for her. I just don't know how to fix the way she's feeling, but hopefully once Liam is finally caught, she can get back to her old self again.

"Okay, now that we have sorted everything out here, why don't we spend the day doing a little bit of shopping. Get you some new clothes and you can find some bits for the house to put your touch on things". Her face lights up a little at the idea of shopping, and so I put the car into drive, and we go to the closest mall, where she gets a few things for herself, and we pick up some new bits for the house too. I thought she would have gone crazy in the clothing stores, but she just got herself a few bits.

After a couple of hours, we finally make it back to the house, I unload the bags and when inside I dump them on the floor, collapsing on the sofa. Grace flops down next to me seemingly exhausted by the day's activities too, as she moves herself over to cuddle up to me. "God that was a long ass day, I remember why I hate shopping so much". I laugh a little, cuddling up to her too, "Yeah I thought you would have got more than you did to be honest". She looks up at me, brow scrunched a little, "Jaxx, I have enough to see me through, I know you wouldn't let me spend my own money so I didn't get a lot on purpose, I will get more eventually but I'm not spending your money just because I needed new bits, and once I am back working again I'll get more, and I might even treat you too".

I smile down to her, pressing my lips gently to hers, and when I pull back her eyes are closing a little, and I watch her for a moment as she fights sleep. "Why don't we have a little nap before dinner, you must be exhausted after today". She yawns a little as I say that, so there's no denying that she actually needs the rest today. "Okay but can we stay here? I'm comfy and don't want to move".

I snuggle into her more, pulling her on top of me so we're both lying down on the sofa, “Of course baby girl”. We fall asleep on the sofa together and end up sleeping the rest of the afternoon away, my phone on silent and long forgotten making me miss a few calls from Harris.

36

Grace

My nightmares wake me again for what feels like the hundredth night in a row. I sit up sweating, cold and clammy like I have done every night since the fire. The police are still looking for Liam even though he was spotted two weeks ago, but he seems to have disappeared off the radar again. I want to not worry about it, but the longer he goes without being found, the more I think he is going to come back for me to try and finish the job.

"Grace, baby are you alright? Did you have another nightmare?" Jaxx's sleepy voice drifts up from beside me, and as I look down at him, a wave of guilt hits me—I've woken him up again. "Jaxx go back to sleep, I'm sorry I didn't mean to wake you". He flicks the lamp on, sitting up and turns to face me, a frown shadow's his sleepy features, "Grace, don't apologise for waking me up, I want to comfort you and if you aren't sleeping then I won't be sleeping either. I'll go make us something to drink, do you want to stay in bed or come downstairs for a little while?" God this man, I give him a small smile before replying "I'll stay in bed if that's okay?" he returns my smile with a soft and warm one of his own, leaning in he presses a light kiss to my lips, “Okay, I’ll be back up shortly” he climbs out of bed, throws on some sweats and heads down-stairs to make us something to drink.

I let out a sigh, lying back against the pillows, sleep now long forgotten as my mind is filled with every scenario of Liam finding me again, but I'm soon pulled from my thoughts again as Jaxx comes back into the room. He's holding something hot up to me and I take it from him, bringing it to my nose and inhaling the scent. “Mmm hot chocolate, thank you” I say smil-ing up to him and sipping on the milky drink. He comes to sit back in bed next to me with his own in hand, looking a little concerned. I glance back over to him, letting out a sigh and rolling my eyes a little, as I feel him watching my every move. “Jaxx I’m fine honestly, stop watching me like I'm going to have a mental breakdown”.

He places his mug on the side table and turns to me, taking my free hand in both of his. I realise that this isn't going to be a light and easy conversation that he's about to spew out to me, so I put my own drink down too and give him my full attention. “Grace, I am only saying this because I love you and I want to help you get back to your normal self soon”, I open my mouth to interrupt him, but he holds his hand up silenc-ing me, “Just let me finish what I need to say”, I nod allowing him to continue. Letting out a long breath, he closes his eyes briefly before beginning, “I know you feel like you are fine, and to other people you put on a good front, but that’s in the daytime and at night I watch you struggle with your nightmares. I think it might be a good idea for you to go and see someone and talk to them, see if it helps".

I frown at him, trying to get my head around what he's saying. "So you think that I need to see a therapist, is that what you're saying?" He sees the frustration from his comment on my face, and shakes his head a little, "Don't be angry with me for suggesting it, I just want you to speak to someone and see if that helps with sleeping at night, because there's only so long you can carry on like this. I got a number for someone in town, and no one will need to know if you don't want them to, but I can see what a toll this is taking on you and I don't enjoy watching it".

I let out a small sigh, slumping back in the pillows again and letting my eyes close briefly. I know he's right; I left my job almost two weeks ago and have made no effort to sort out my new job with my dad and brother, I'm just surviving off the savings in my bank account. Jaxx hasn't pushed me to start my new role yet either, but I know it must be hard on him too.

Opening my eyes, I look over to him and give him a tight smile, watching as his eyes soften towards me, and I know I need to do the right thing for the both of us. "Okay, give me the number, I'll set up an appointment and go this week, and I know I need to get back to work too so I'll speak to Tristan about getting started soon", "I don't want you to feel like you need to start your new job right away, let's just get started with one thing at a time, and we'll take it from there. If you feel like you want to still start after your first session, then call your brother". I lean over and snuggle into him, his arms coming around me, bringing back that sense of comfort I crave so much right now. “Thank you Jaxx. I know it’s a lot for you too, and I want to do what I can to get back to normal soon”. He kisses the top of my head, before resting his chin there, “I know baby girl. We'll get you back to your best in no time, I just don't want to see you suffering any-more”.

I look up to him and lean in to press a kiss to his lips, pulling back a little when I feel him smiling back against my lips, a cheeky grin tugging up at his lips. “Since we're up and I'm now very wide awake, I think we should wear each other out a little, don't you?” I giggle back to him using a kiss as my reply, allowing it to deepen more than before, and then pull back a little, my lips brushing against his, “Hmm I think that sounds like a good idea”. His hands come up to roam over my body, as the magic they seem to con-tain helps me to forget what even woke me in the first place.

He's a lot more gentle with me tonight than usual, slow and measured like he's pouring all his love into this moment, keeping me close to him, his kisses tender and gentle as he lazily pushes himself into me, moving at a pace that’s both torture and amazing all at once. We move together slowly, building a rhythm that soon brings us both to our release, his hand coming be-tween us as he uses his skilled fingers to brush against my clit, giving me that extra bit I need to get me there. We don't speak, we don't need words to tell each other how much we need this right now.

As he always does once we finish, he goes to the bathroom bringing back a warm cloth to clean me up, and then climbs back into bed with me, pulling me close to him again, pressing his lips to my temple as sleep takes over for the remainder of the night, and for the first time since the fire, I finally feel like things could eventually get better.

37

Grace

The brick building I'm standing in front of should intimidate me, a few years ago it probably would have. But today, all I feel is a sense of calm, knowing I might finally start to begin building myself up to be me again, not the old me, but a new improved version that doesn't take shit from anyone. I drove myself here today, for the first time in weeks I decided I needed to start doing things for myself. Liam is still missing, and I have grown fed up with being in hiding constantly and I forced Jaxx to go back to work because he was desperately needed at the station, he begrudgingly agreed eventually and went back last week.

My sister and mom have both been on hand to be close by in case I needed it, and even though at times I felt like I did I didn't want to seem like I was being needy, so I didn't bother them, but right now I feel like I need someone to give me that little push I need to get inside. As I'm standing with my thought's, staring into space an older lady approaches me, she's got kind eyes and a warm smile, dressed in Jeans and a jumper. Coming to stand next to me, she's quiet for a moment before she speaks, "You know this is really the hardest part.

The easy bit I find is talking, but I'm guessing you already know that since you haven't yet made an attempt to walk up the stairs yet".

I blink back at her, "Oh um" I say pointing towards the building "I am going in, I just wanted to collect my thoughts, do you work here?" Her hand comes out to shake mine, "Melanie James, I'm one of the therapists here". I smile as I shake her hand, "I think I'm actually seeing you today, so it's nice to meet you. I'm Grace Vale". She's giving off good vibes, and it's making me look forward to today. "Great, nice to meet you, Grace. Let's head inside and get settled then, if you'd like to follow me".

....

I come out of therapy feeling lighter than I ever have in years, and I think I learned more about myself in that hour than I have done going through my entire adult life. We went into a little more detail about my nightmares and what triggered them, and she gave me some coping mechanisms to try and help stop them. As I head back to my car, I pull my phone out and call Jaxx to tell him I've left as he asked me to check in with him. We're chatting for a minute when someone comes to stop right in front of me, causing me to bump into them. "Excuse me, you literally just..." My sentence dies in my throat as the person staring back to me is no stranger at all. "Grace, are you okay?" I hear Jaxx say down the phone but all I can do is try to control my breathing as Liam stares me in the face, finger to his lips.

My breathing becomes more ragged, and Jaxx seems to pick up on the fact I'm in trouble, because well I'm in deep shit if he doesn't figure out I need help without me speaking. He speaks quietly into the phone, hoping I can still hear him and no one else, "Grace say something, anything if you need help and I can be with you in a couple of minutes". I cough into the phone, but Liam seems to pick up on the fact that whoever is on the other end of the phone knows I'm in trouble. "Hang up the phone", Liam says to me. His gruff voice is barely above a whisper but threatening all the same, and because I'm an idiot, I say "okay Liam I'm hanging up now" so Jaxx knows just how much shit I'm in, the phone is quickly ripped from my hands, as Liam grabs it, hanging up and tossing it to the side.

Fear grips at me but I try not to show it as I square my shoulders and level my gaze with his. "What do you want Liam? You do know there's a warrant out for your arrest, right? I have people watching me, so you need to leave". The lie slips from my lips easily and I realise I am basically helping him get away, but right now I'll say just about anything to make him leave me alone. He shakes his head laughing a little at me, and as he starts to walk towards me, I take a step back, each step matching his until I'm backed up against a wall and have little to no room to make an escape. I need to stall as much as I possibly can, but I'm very quickly running out of ideas and so I try the talking tactic again, the adrenaline running through me helping with the confidence "Why are you going to such extreme lengths to hurt me? Did you ever even love me at all?" He stalls for a second, caught off guard by my question, and part of me wonders if he even knows why he's going to the lengths he is.

"You are meant to be with me, no one else. I asked you to come home and you ignored my requests, so I had to take matters into my own hands and that's why I came to bring you back, but then you tell me that you're over me so soon, and with some other guy". I hold up my hands to stop him, is he seriously hearing himself right now? "Liam, I'd still be with you if you didn't cheat on me, I don't understand why you're acting so hurt about this when it was you who caused the whole situation". He pulls back, shaking his head and grabbing at his hair a little. A tell of his frustration I picked up on a while back. "Grace, I did that because you were pushing me away, I needed to know you cared about me".

A laugh bursts out of me, he actually sounds delusional right now. I really am beginning to think he may have had some sort of a breakdown from the way he's relaying this story to me, like it's actually making sense to him in his head. I try to get my bearings a little and stop myself from laughing at him, but it just keeps coming out, which doesn't do me any favours because it just makes him angrier.

I'm pulled from my laughing fit when his hands grip tightly against my shoulders as he shoves me back up against the wall, winding me a little as he does and causing me to catch my head off the brick. I cry out but it does nothing to help me right now as he gets in my face, his own now void of any emotion. I try to look him straight in the eye to hide any fear I feel but when I look back to him, his blue eyes are hollow and dead. I let my gaze slide over his face, getting a good look on his features. He looks like he's lost weight, his cheekbones now hollowed out, and that sun kissed glow he used to have has gone, his skin now a dull greying colour. He looks rough, and I wonder if he really is okay.

He goes to speak but the second he does, another voice filters in from behind us, “Lay one more finger on her and I swear I will blow your goddamn head off. Put your hands in the air and back away slowly”. Liam’s eyes momentarily widen in fear right in front of me, and I think he may have just had a crashing dose of reality drench him like a bucket of ice water over his head.

For once he does as he’s told and begins backing away from me, not quickly enough though it seems, as he is suddenly dragged backwards and down onto the ground. My eyes shoot up meeting with Jaxx's for a split second before his eyes move to the floor where Liam is currently being cuffed by another police officer. He's dragged up from the floor pretty quickly and read his rights as the police officer walks him back to the waiting car.

My brain decides that’s the time to shut off, as I feel myself start to go lightheaded. I sway a little staggering forward, and the motion catches Jaxx’s attention causing him to dart towards me, reaching me just before I hit the floor, “You're okay baby girl, I've got you now”. I feel his fingers stroke over my hair, and I give him the best smile I can muster up, right before the adrenaline in my body gives out, causing me to pass out from the shock.

38

Jaxx

Seeing Grace faint in front of me brings me back to the night of the fire again. Her body limp and lifeless as I cradle her in my arms, I pull her keys from her pocket and lift her up, walking us to her car. I know deep down that she's going to be okay, but I decide to take her to the hospital anyway just in case he did do anything to her that I wasn't aware of. Putting her into the passenger seat, I strap her in while she's still passed out and make the short journey to the hospital.

Carrying her inside in my work uniform seems to help with the speed of her being seen to, as she's placed on a gurney and sent into resus quickly, and I'm back in the waiting area staring at my phone trying to figure out what to say to her brother for the second time in a few short weeks. Scrolling through my contacts, I find Tristan's number and tap his name. I'm surprised he answers so quickly since it's the middle of the day, "Hey Jaxx everything alright?"

I suppress the urge to let out a groan, because no. No everything is not alright, "Err, yeah and no. Do you want the good or the bad news first?" Tristan actually does let out a groan as he complains down the phone, "Ahh fuck Jaxx what has happened now?" I blow out a long breath, my elbows resting on my knees as I rub at my brow, trying to stop the headache that's fast approaching. "So, we finally got Liam, he cornered grace whilst she was out and..."

Tristan cuts me off before I can get out what I need to, "Woah, hold on. Why the fuck was Grace out by herself when you hadn't yet found him? I thought we had all agreed we'd stay with her until he was caught". Fucks sake. "Really that's what you pick up on out of that sentence? She was at an appointment and had insisted on going alone as she didn't want anyone to know where she was going, and don't ask me questions about it because I am not going to tell you. She rang me when she left though, and I was on the phone to her when it happened. We got to him before he could do anything, and he's now been arrested".

He's quiet for a moment, typical that he doesn't talk when I need him to, but after what seems like forever he eventually speaks again, "Okay so that's the good news, what's the bad news?" *Please don't kill me for saying this,* "Grace is um, well I brought her to the hospital because she fainted, and I wanted to get her checked over". "Ahh for fucks sake man. Do I need to come to the hospital? Are they keeping her in? I'll tell mom and dad". Jesus this guy is a mile a minute right now, "Tris, slow the fuck down, you'll give yourself an aneurism if you carry on. I don't think you'll need to come to the hospital, she just passed out and I'm being over cautious, we should be home by tonight if you want to give her a call, but I think it might be best that you let her relax at least for tonight, yeah? I'll keep you updated as much as I can".

He blows out a breath down the phone, before responding, “Alright man. Keep me updated as best as you can, and I'll let mom and dad know”. We hang up after that, and I get to my feet pacing the floor. It feels like they are taking forever in there and I need something to distract myself from going through every worst-case scenario, and so I head over to the coffee machine and order myself a drink.

I’m waiting another thirty minutes before someone comes out to speak to me. A male doctor approaches me, his facial features give nothing away though so I’m unsure if he's about to deliver me good or bad news. Bracing for either, I stand as he nears, holding out my hand for him to shake. “Good afternoon I’m Dr Young, I've been dealing with Grace today, and I wanted to come and give you the update. She’s woken back up and was complaining of a headache, so I’ve ordered an MRI just to be on the safe side, but she seems to just have a mild concussion. I've given her some pain relief and provided the scan comes back clear she'll be good to go home”.

I breathe out a sigh of relief knowing she's going to be alright, “Thank you for looking after her, am I okay to go in and see her now?” Nodding to me, with a ghost of a smile to his lips, he shows me through to where Grace is, and once again I'm floored at the sight of her. Tear-stained cheeks that I wasn’t here to catch when they fell from her eyes. To the red rimmed eyes that hold so much emotion right now. When those Green eyes catch mine though, all the sadness disappears from them, and the love that she gives me every day pours out of her as she holds her arms out to me. I go straight to her and pull her so tightly against me she gasps a little. “Jaxx, your grip is a little tight”, she breathes the words into my ear, and I relax a tiny bit, the feeling of her back in my arms calming me again.

I pull back to get a good look at her again, my hands coming up to her face, cupping either side so I have her full attention “Grace, I'm so sorry, I let you down today. I told you I wouldn't let anything happen to you again and here I am back messing that very thing up”. Her eyes shine up at me, glistening with more unshed tears that threaten to fall down her face. One slips free and my thumb swipes across her delicate cheek to take it away, her eyes flutter a little at the movement, and as the feeling to be as close to her as I can overtakes me, I move in closer to her, brushing my lips against hers, before pressing a little more firmly against them. She leans into the kiss too and I pour everything I have into it, I need to show her she will be safe with me, because I really will go to the ends of the earth to protect her.

We pull away from each other, just sitting watching our movements for a moment, her eyes dart between mine before she finally speaks “I'm okay Jaxx, I promise. Nothing happened to me and now Liam has finally been arrested, I can get back to normal. I want to feel like I don't have to worry anymore, and I feel like what’s happened today might just be the steppingstone to that”. My head comes to rest against hers and I close my eyes as I soak in what she's just said to me. “I know Grace, but I just feel like I've let you down. When you.. When you called me today and I heard his voice over the phone, I really thought that I wouldn't get to you in time. I'm just thankful that I was as close as I was when you rang me, I think I subconsciously made sure to stay close to where you were in case, I needed to get to you fast”.

Her gentle voice filters through my ears, lifting my mood that little bit more, “Jaxx, please stop worrying now, I’m fine and I'd actually really like to go home”. I shake my head at her a little and she scowls back at me. “Sorry baby girl, but no can do just yet, you need a scan because you told the doctors you hit your head, and I'm not about to take any risks and break you out of here, so can you stay put just a little longer and then we can go home?”

Grace peaks up at me through her thick lashes, a small smile playing across her rosy pink lips. “Only if you promise to make me a grilled cheese when we get home”. I lean down, pecking at her lips before replying, “Anything for you princess”.

....

By the time we make it back home, it’s past four in the afternoon, the winter nights kicking in as it’s almost dark outside. I pull on to the drive and when I look over to Grace, she's fallen asleep during the twenty-minute journey from the hospital. She looks so peaceful right now that I almost don’t want to wake her up, but we can't stay in the car all evening, so I get out and round to her side, lifting her out as gently as I can as to not wake her, she stirs a little in my arms but settles almost instantly against my chest as I carry her inside.

I take her into the living room and lay her on the couch so I can head into the kitchen and make us some food. I'm only in there a minute or two though when my phone starts ringing, and when I pull it out I see Tristan's name on my screen, I answer the call, putting the phone to my ear, "Hey, sorry we literally just walked in the door and I'm about to make some food, Grace is asleep so I will get her to call you back when she's awake". I say to him, and he replies to me instantly, "Oh yeah that's fine, I just wanted to check as I called her a couple of times and there was no answer". I think for a minute and realise I haven't heard her phone ring, quickly remembering that Liam took it off her, "Ahh shit, I think hers was taken from her by Liam earlier, I'll call up the station and see if they found it when we left". We talk some more on the phone, and eventually I hang up and shoot a text over to one of the officers that were on duty today, I'm only waiting for a minute or so when a reply comes back in letting me know they picked up Grace's phone at the scene, but the screen was cracked on it, and I make a mental note to get that fixed for her.

I reply my thanks and get to work making us the grilled cheese she requested, and by the time they're ready, Grace comes wandering into the kitchen still looking half asleep. I hold my arm out to her and she comes around the island to my side, leaning into me whilst I wait for the sandwiches to finish off. I press a kiss to her head before speaking, "Why don't you go make us a drink, this is almost ready". She nods into me, and I release her as she sleepily walks over to the fridge to make herself and me a drink.

We sit and eat in comfortable silence and once finished, I head upstairs to make her a bath, lighting the candles in the bathroom and putting a towel on the heater for her, before returning downstairs to see her sitting, staring into space. I go up to her as carefully as I can, placing my hands gently on her shoulders and rubbing up and down her arms a little. She moves a little, but the action doesn't cause her to jump, "I've run you a bath, you go upstairs and have a soak and I'll clean up down here.

She nods at me absently, heading upstairs to take a bath and I head into the living room, grabbing a beer on the way. I relax into the sofa, taking a sip from my beer, and after a moment I close my eyes to just think. Thank fuck he's finally been found. I know it's going to be a long journey ahead for her, but I will make sure she never has to go anywhere near a court-room anytime soon.

39

Grace

The two weeks following Liam's arrest go by in a blur. He was charged without bail for multiple charges and will thankfully be spending a long time behind bars, not just for what he did to me, but for a whole plethora of things, including hacking into banking systems and the systems at his company, he's going down for attempted murder alongside fraud. Turns out he had stolen a couple of hundred thousand from the business he'd been working at for years and had been putting the money into another account, presumably so that he could disappear easily. But what goes around comes around, and for people like him, I'm slowly coming to the realisation that he deserves everything he's got coming his way.

Today is a good day and the start of a whole new journey for me though, as I'm about to start my first day as a part of the Meadow Creek ranch team, working alongside my brother and for the time being, my dad also. We hashed out a few details a few weeks earlier, but Tristan and I made the decision that we would run the ranch as a whole new enterprise, starting as it is now and expanding over the next few years. My sister Lily has straight up said she wants nothing to do with it but wants her kids to have the option to join the family business when the time comes, it was easy enough to agree to that and she doesn't know it yet, but she is a small shareholder of the company and will get her first cheque on Christmas day.

It's only a couple of weeks before Christmas and my dad had said I could start in the new year, but I wanted to get started as soon as I could. I was itching to get back to work and since my nightmares were beginning to only come every once in a while, I was able to get a few good nights of sleep in.

As I pull up the drive, I'm greeted by all the Christmas decorations my mom has gone to town on. Lights trail down the drive, draped over the fencing along the way, lighting a path to the stables and barn. She's had lights put everywhere, and as much as I love it, the whole house is so over the top. My mom spots me as I get out of the car, and comes running down the steps from the front door to greet me, "Grace honey, how are you my sweet girl?" She asks as she wraps me up in her arms, god I've missed her hugs all the time, and I'm so glad to be here with her as much as I can until they go off on their travels in the new year. My dad trusts us both enough that we won't kill each other, and so they pulled their plans forward by a few weeks, heading out the 2nd week of January.

"I'm good mom, I'm just glad to be back at work, and I'm caffeinated enough that I won't kill Tristan in the first half of the day. I can't make any promises for this afternoon though". I slide her a grin, winking at her so she at least knows I'm kind of joking, I would at least wait until they've left before I murder him.

My dad comes walking out the door a minute after my mom does, coming over to give me a hug before handing me over a freshly brewed cup of coffee, he knows me too well. "C'mon kiddo, let's get you settled into your new office before I head out for the rest of the day. I've kept Tristan busy enough that he won't be a bother to you for at least a week". He shoots me a wink as he says it, and I know he's probably sent him as far away from me as he can whilst I get my bearings at work.

I follow him down to the newly refurbished barn, which has been converted into a new office space, and find that I've been given one of the offices with the most amazing view looking over the paddocks, the sunshine rising over the east, so I'll have the sun shining into my room the whole day. He turns to me smiling, "This was going to be my office, but since I'm leaving soon, I decided you could have it. You'll be in the office a hell of a lot more than Tristan, so you deserve it". He throws me another wink as I make my way around to my new office chair, coming to a halt as I spot sunflowers on my desk. I beam up at my dad for being so thoughtful, but he shakes his head at me, a small smile touching his lips as he points to the bouquet on my desk. "Those aren't from me sweetheart, Jaxx called your mom up and had her put them in here yesterday, so you had something to keep you in a good mood for the day".

I beam even more at that, my heart warming even more that Jaxx was so thoughtful and did that for me, my dad makes his excuses to leave and I'm left staring out of the new view from my office, my mood hitting the best it's been for weeks thanks to this sweet start to my day, I take in the stunning view for a moment more before deciding to send a text to Jaxx thanking him.

ME: Thank you for the flowers. Day officially made. I love you xxx

He responds not a minute later, and I know I have a keeper for life.

JAXX: I will keep them coming for the rest of your life baby girl, have a great first day. I love you xxx

Epilogue

Jaxx

6 months later

"Grace, hurry up and get your ass downstairs, we're gonna be late", I shout up the stairs, hoping it might just spur her on the tiniest bit, but all it seems to do is anger my girlfriend even more, "Jaxx shut the fuck up. I had to spend the morning putting everything back together after the dog *you* wanted decided to destroy the house. I'll be ready soon", Grace's silky voice projects down the stairs and I suppress the urge to laugh, looking down to our new Golden Retriever Honey, who's currently trying to chew through one of Grace's vans. "Shit" I murmur to myself as I try and pry the shoe from her mouth. She thinks it's a game, but I'm sure Grace will sell her if she catches the dog eating another item of her clothing.

I scoop the pup up into my arms and wander out to the backyard so she can run off some of her energy whilst we wait for Grace to emerge. Grace is another ten minutes before she comes wandering out to see us, waiting at the back door with her phone in one hand and a very chewed shoe in the other. She's looking absolutely stunning in a sage green sundress that's dotted with flowers, her hair in loose waves around her face, and a pair of vans on her feet as usual. I have to remember to keep my dick in check today, because I've got big plans for him later.

I'm pulled from my thoughts though when Grace launches the shoe at me and yells across the yard, “You owe me a new pair”, then turns to saunter back in the house, Honey hot on her heels, and not a care in the world that she just nearly knocked me out.

I catch up to her quickly, wrapping an arm around her waist as I pull her back towards me, her back flush against my chest. “You know, assault on an officer is a serious offence, baby girl” I murmur into her ear as my grip tightens a little around her waist, she peaks up at me through her mascara clad lashes, blinking a couple of times, as if she doesn't know I'm on to her innocent act. “Well then, said officer shouldn't let his dog eat my fucking shoe. It was warranted”. Her lips tilt up into a smirk as she pulls herself away from me, spinning half a turn to face me as I grab her by the waist again and pull her close.

My lips brush up against hers for a moment as I inhale her floral scent, enjoying the moment before we need to get to her parents for a barbeque. “I'll buy you ten pairs if you want, and I promise I'll get some training for Honey”. Grace smiles back up to me as I give in and press my lips to hers, savouring the softness of them against mine. Our intimate moment is quickly interrupted though when Honey barks from beside us, reminding us that we need to leave. “I think that’s our queue to leave now”.

Honey wanders out of the house and to the car, following behind Grace whilst I lock up and check my pockets one final time, making sure I have absolutely everything I need, we get on the road heading over to her parents' place.

The sun is beating down in the sky, and for June it's a little on the warmer side, but we're making the most of it, as her parents are back for the week taking a break from their travels to spend a little time with the family. We arrive after everyone else as usual; it seems we get nowhere fast recently, but I am looking forward to spending time with my best friend and my girl's family again for the first time in so long.

Everyone is out back enjoying drinks, and as Grace is greeting her family, I slink off to grab a beer with Tristan. Honey has long forgotten who we are as the kids play on the grass with her. The two other golden retrievers of her parents, enjoying the play with the new addition.

....

Grace

Jaxx disappears off with my brother for another little secret chat, which they seem to be doing a lot of lately, and I'm trying not to get suspicious, but my curiosity gets the better of me. I'm about to follow them and be nosey, but my sister calls me over to help her with max, as he's doing a runner with the dog down the garden. I chase after the pair, finally grabbing them both, Max's giggles reminding me why I love these family days so much. We make our way back up the garden and my sister calls out to me to bring Max to her. I'm with them for a couple of minutes when Jaxx shouts me over to help with the dog, *Christ do I not get a rest today.*

He's holding honey and messing with something that seems to be stuck to her, "Can you give me a hand, she's got something around her neck". Bringing the dog down to my level, I try to remove whatever she's somehow managed to get tangled in, but when I finally get it off, I notice it's a ribbon with a tiny trinket box attached to it.

Jaxx put's Honey back down on the floor and takes the box from me, kneeling down on one knee in front of me and popping the little trinket box open. My mouth pops open with it as I take in the beautiful ring in front of me, my wide eyes jumping up to meet those beautiful steely grey ones that make my heart melt every time I look into them. He looks nervous right now, but I remember to keep my mouth shut for a minute, bringing my hands up to cover it, more from shock than anything.

"Grace, having known you almost my entire life, once as my best friends annoying little sister, and now the love of my life, I'm certain I wouldn't want to relive a moment of the years we have spent winding each other up or the past nine months, no matter how difficult times may have been. You are my absolute world, and I don't think I can go another minute without asking you. So, will you please do me the honour of becoming my wife".

I blink back down to him, lost for words. I can't even form a sentence right now, so I fall to my knees in front of him, nodding eagerly and throwing my arms around him. His arms come to wrap around my waist, squeezing me back just as hard as I am him, murmuring in my ear, he asks “Is that a yes baby girl?” I pull back, nodding some more, tears pouring down my face as I take his own face into my hands, “Yes Jaxx a thousand times yes!” He pulls my left hand away from his face, bringing it down to place the solitaire ring on my finger. My family cheers around us as I throw my arms back around his neck and he lifts us, squeezing me tightly, as he whispers in my ear, “I've got you baby girl, forever.”

Next in the series, Need you.

To read Rose and Luca’s story, check out my socials for updates on the release.

@robynreedsbooks

About the author.

Robyn works full time as a fully qualified nail technician, and lives in Cheshire, England with her husband Jacob and their Labrador Jack. When she isn't at the salon or out with the dog, you can find her at home, with her head in a good spicy romance novel.

Printed in Great Britain
by Amazon

52536872R00175